Early Life Leadership Research

WHERE DO LEADERS COME FROM?

Exploring the Relationship Between Personality and Leadership Skills in Kindergarten Students

CHRISTINA DEMARA

All Rights Reserved

Early Life Leadership for Children: Where do leaders come from?

Published by DeMara-Kirby & Associates, LLC.
P.O. Box 720335 McAllen, Texas 78572

© 2017 Christina DeMara

U.S. Copyright Office, 2019

All material in Early Life Leadership for Children: Where do leaders come from?, including all intellectual ideas, methodology, materials, pictures, and graphics on these pages, are copyrighted by DeMara-Kirby & Associates.

All rights and intellectual property reserved. No part of these pages, either text or image, may be used for any purpose other than personal use. Therefore, presentation, reproduction, modification, storage in a retrieval system, or retransmission, in any form or by any means, electronic, mechanical, without written permission from the author is prohibited without prior written permission from DeMara-Kirby & Associates and Christina DeMara. General inquiries should be directed to christinademara.com.

DISCLAIMER:

Early Life Leadership for Children: Where do leaders come from? is based on the research, professional opinion, and experiences of the author, and it does not promise anything to the reader. All permissions needed for this study were granted. The author is simply publishing this research to bring awareness of leadership skills with children.

Table of Contents

1: Where Do Leaders Come From? 5
    Early Life Leadership Reflections 14
    Early Life Leadership Notes 15

2: The Mind and Foundation of a Child 16
    Early Life Leadership Reflections 22
    Early Life Leadership Notes 23

3: Early Life Leadership Research 24
    Early Life Leadership Reflections 27
    Early Life Leadership Notes 30

4: What Does Research Say? 31
    Early Life Leadership Reflections 86
    Early Life Leadership Notes 87

5: Research Procedure 88
    Early Life Leadership Notes 100

6: Results 101
    Did previous formal schooling have an effect on children's leadership skills? 109
    Did gender have an effect on children's leadership skills? 110
    Did language have an effect on children's leadership skills? 111
    Relationship Between Surveys and Personality Variables 112

    Early Life Leadership Notes 121

7: Research Findings 122

    Discussion of Findings.. 122

    Summary of Findings 124

    What Does This Research Imply? 127

    Early Life Leadership Notes 133

8: So, Where Do Leaders Come From? 134

    Early Life Leadership Notes 136

Christina DeMara's Book Catalog

If you love learning and leadership, you will enjoy:

Igniting Leadership
50 Research-Based Strategies for Life and Work

Cultivating Soft Skills

The Power of Leadership Reflection
Higher-Level Thinking Questions and Journaling

My Development Journal

Also Written By Christina DeMara

Peace Is Mine
The Forgiveness Journal

I'm Not Broken
The Power of Prayer, Scripture, and Interactive Journaling

I Will Not Fall
The Power of Prayer, Scripture, and Interactive Journaling

How God Saved Me
My Mother's Memoirs on Abuse, Depression, & Overeating

How God Healed Me
My Mother's Memoirs on Grace, Health, Gastric Bypass & Reconstructive Surgery

The I Am Journal
A Soul-Searching Journal for Creative Women of God

Isaiah 43:2
40 Days of Scriptures, Reflection, and Journaling for the Lent Season

Meaningful Books & Resources

Meaningful Leadership
How to Build Indestructible Relationships with Your Team Members through Intentionality and Faith

Meaningful Leadership Journal

Meaningful Leadership Prayer Journal

Meaningful Teacher Leadership
Reflection, Refinement, and Student Achievement

Meaningful Writing & Self-Publishing
Your Guide to Igniting Your Pen, Faith, Creativity & Entrepreneurship

Early Life LeadershipBooks & Resources

Early Life Leadership Research
Where do leaders come from?

Early Life Leadership in Children
101 Strategies to Grow Great Leaders

Early Life Leadership
101 Conversation Starters and Writing Prompts

Early Life Leadership Workbook
101 Strategies to Grow Great Leaders

Early Life Leadership Workbook for Girls
101 Strategics to Grow Great Leaders

Early Life Leadership Kids Journal

Early Life Leadership in the Classroom
Resources, Strategies & Tidbits to Grow Great Leaders

1: Where Do Leaders Come From?

Many years ago, I was a Special Education teacher. My principal saw something special in me and mentored and encouraged me to go back to school to get my credentials to be an educational administrator. I had never thought of myself as a leader, but I performed well in tasks he gave me, and the challenge satisfied me. I started a new chapter in my life and undertook my master's degree in educational administration. I started this program with a cohort of individuals, all with different aspirations but the similar goal of receiving our masters. I felt a bit intimidated not being the most established, but I was eager to learn. After my first semester, I reflected on how we had started off in a class of twenty-five and ended with eighteen. This led me to question *"Why do some leaders prevail?"* and *"Where do leaders come from?"* I analyzed my elementary school experiences—both personal and professional—more closely in an attempt to answer this.

As I continued my journey, I felt the need to conduct a study to identify the relationship between leadership skills and personality traits in kindergarten students, because I could see leadership traits appearing even in the smallest of children both in the classroom and on the playground. Currently, while there is an abundance of studies published on leadership in adults, very little is known about leadership in children.

This was an IRB (Institution Review Board) approved study. My goal was to build on an existing understanding by analyzing classroom teachers' perception of leadership skills in kindergarten students, and how the presence of these skills connects to a student's personality.

Research Question: *Is there a relationship between leadership skills and personality traits in kindergarten students?*

The surveys used to measure these traits and skills were the *Leadership Skills Checklist* (Castillo, 2001*)* and the *Big Five Personality Traits Inventory* (Goldberg, 1981*)* which established if these skills were more present in children with certain personalities. Teachers completed both surveys based on how they perceive each student because the kindergarteners themselves were too young to participate successfully in a research study.

Besides looking at the relationship between leadership skills and personality traits alone, I hypothesized that there would be some differences between the children discussed in this study that may impact how they displayed both leadership skills and certain personality traits. Those differences are often called controlled variables (or CVs). In this study, I monitored for the effects of:

1. **A child's previous formal schooling (Preschool, Pre-kindergarten, Daycare)**

Do children who start school earlier possess more leadership skills?

I felt that this might affect the behavior of the kindergarteners (either positively or negatively), which in turn would give the teacher a different perception of them, so I asked if they had been previously enrolled in pre-kinder, preschool, or daycare.

2. **Gender**

Does gender make a difference in leadership? Who's the strong leader, girls or boys? (Is there even a difference?)

I believed gender would also be a factor. From this, I posited important sub-questions such as does being one particular gender make for stronger leaders. To address this, the teachers were asked whether the student in question was a girl or boy.

3. **Language (Spanish/bilingual)**

In South Texas where we are predominantly Hispanic, does language have an effect on how teachers see their students as leaders?

I pondered if the language would affect the outcome as the study was carried

out in South Texas where the population is predominantly Hispanic. Would language matter? Taking this into account, I asked teachers to indicate whether the child they

evaluated was bilingual or not.

Conceptual Definitions

Big Five Inventory (BFI): *The Big Five Inventory* (BFI) is a self-report inventory designed to measure *The Big Five Personality Traits*. It is a multidimensional personality inventory (consisting of 44 items in total) and consists of short phrases with relatively accessible vocabulary (Srivastava, 2015).

Big Five Personality Traits: Five dimensions of personality traits

(1) Extraversion: includes the talkative, energetic, and assertive traits (Srivastava, 2015)

(2) Agreeableness: includes sympathetic, kind, and affectionate traits (Srivastava, 2015)

(3) Conscientiousness: includes organization, thoroughness, and self-awareness (Srivastava, 2015)

(4) Neuroticism (sometimes reversed and called Emotional Stability): includes tension, moodiness, and anxiety (Srivastava, 2015)

(5) Openness to Experience (sometimes called Intellect or Intellect/Imagination): includes having multiple interests, imaginativeness, and insightfulness (Srivastava, 2015).

Early Childhood (age): The early stage of growth and development for a child age two to eight (Junn & Boyztzis, 1996).

Early Childhood Education: A term referring to educational programs and strategies geared toward children zero to eight. Based on the research and philosophy of Jean Piaget (2013), early childhood education often focuses on learning through play.

Gifted and Talented: A term used to describe children who convey outstanding talent and demonstrate the potential to achieve remarkably high levels of accomplishment when compared with other children who share the same age, experience level, or environment as them (US Department of Education, 1993).

Bilingual Education: A program for language minority students in the United States running from kindergarten to 12th grade in which both English and the students' native language is used for academic instruction (Geneseem & Paradis, 2004).

English Language Learners (ELLs): Language minority students in the United States who are learning English as the majority language for social integration and educational purpose. Native Spanish-speaking, Vietnamese-speaking, and Korean-speaking children who reside and are educated in the United States would fall into this category, for example. ELLs were previously referred to as Limited English Proficient (LEP) students. This term continues to prevail in federal and state legislation but is not widely used by educators and researchers due to the negative connotations of the term "limited" (Genesee & Paradis, 2004).

Operational Definitions

Causal relationships: In some data sets, it is possible to conclude that one variable has a direct influence on the other. This is called a causal relationship.

Control for a variable: To control for a variable is to try to separate its effect from the treatment effect, so it will not interfere with the treatment. There are many methods that try to control for variables: some methods are based on matching individuals between treatment and control; others use assumptions about the effects of the variables to try to model the effect mathematically, for example, using regression (Stark, 2014).

Correlation: A measure of linear association between two (ordered) lists. Two variables can be strongly correlated without having any causal relationship, and two variables can have a causal relationship and be uncorrelated (Stark, 2014).

Dependent Variable: In regression, the variable whose values are supposed to be explained by changes in the other variable (the independent, or explanatory variable). Usually, one regresses the dependent variable on the independent variable (Stark, 2014).

Independent Variable: In regression, the independent variable is supposed to explain the dependent variable (the term "independent" is a synonym for "explanatory"). Usually, one regresses the dependent variable on the independent variable. There is not always a clear choice of independent variable. The independent variable is usually plotted on the horizontal axis. (Stark, 2014).

Population: A collection of units being studied. These units can be people, places, objects, epochs, drugs, procedures, or many other things. Much of statistics is concerned with estimating the numerical properties (parameters) of an entire population from a random sample of units within it (Stark, 2014).

Regression: A technique for determining the statistical relationship between two or more variables (http://www.businessdictionary.com, 2018).

Read more:

http://www.businessdictionary.com/definition/regression.html

Sample: A collection of units from a population (Stark, 2014).

Sampling distribution: A sampling distribution is a graph of a statistic of your sample data. It is a statistic picture that may display Mean, Mean absolute value of the deviation from the mean, Range, Standard deviation of the sample, Unbiased estimate of variance, and Variance of the sample. The sampling distribution of an applied random sample (Stark, 2014).

T-test: A t-test is a type of inferential statistic which is used to determine if there is a significant difference between the means of two groups (Stark, 2014).

Variable: A numerical value or a characteristic that can differ from individual to individual (Stark, 2014).

Leadership Skills Checklist: This checklist was intended for the classroom teacher to use to identify leadership skills in children. The *Leadership Skills Checklist* identifies nine skills: (1) child has good communication, (2) child is willing to take on extra responsibility, (3) child encourages others' ideas, (4) other students look up to them as a leader, (5) child delegates, (6) child is confident, (7) child is flexible, (8) child is a risk-taker, and (9) child is dependable (Castillo, 2001).

EARLY LIFE LEADERSHIP REFLECTIONS

1. Why is studying leadership important to you?

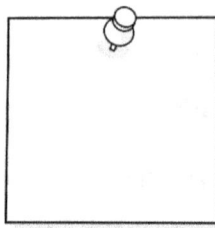

2. How can acknowledging leadership in children change your perspective?

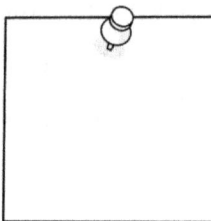

3. Do you think there is a relationship between personality and leadership skills?

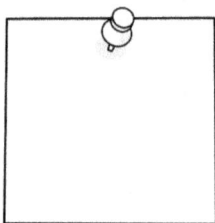

EARLY LIFE LEADERSHIP NOTES

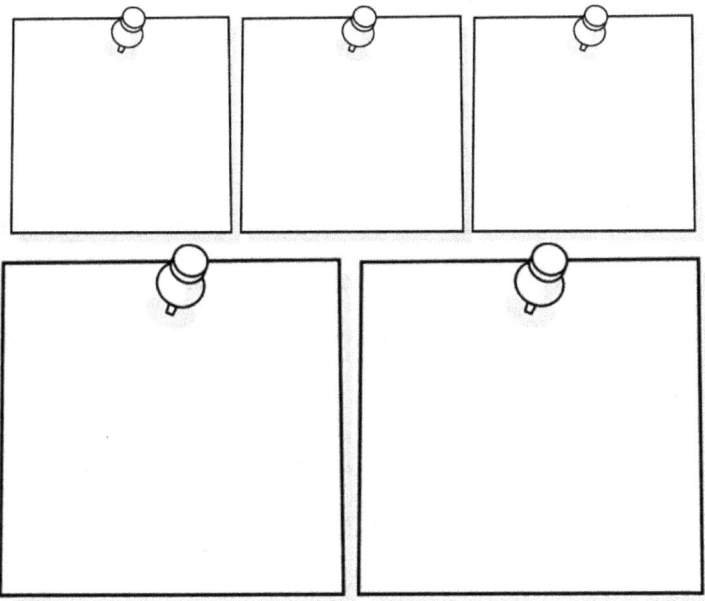

2: The Mind and Foundation of a Child

As most countries have faced financial problems, violence, and tragedy in recent years, leadership has become a global area of interest for reform (Bennis & Goldsmith, 2010). The call for leadership echoes louder and louder, and ignites two questions:

1. *Where and how are leaders being grown and cultivated?*
2. *Can children be taught to lead?*

As we have seen in the previous chapter, the promotion and growth of leadership in children crave exploration (Guthrie, Jones, Hu, & Osteen, 2013), but before that can be done, we must first understand child development and where leadership qualities emerge from.

Early childhood occurs from the ages of 0-8, where learning occurs through play and socialization before the rigor of formal book-and-paper schooling. John Piaget explored the foundation for early cognitive development in small children when he carried out a large-scale study on early cognition and understanding in 1952. He found three processes at work:

1. *Simulation, in which a child demonstrates learned behavior, such as in role play*
2. *Accommodation. in which the child alters this behavior due to lived experience*
3. *Equilibrium, in which a balance is struck between what is originally demonstrated to the child and this altering process*

(Piaget, 1952 & Charlesworth, 1987).

This begs the question, can leadership be taught through social simulations such as role-playing in an educational setting? To attempt to answer this, we need to look at Piaget's work on a deeper level to include the schemas of child learning and brain function, as well as the work of others who have been influenced by his findings and inspired to research theories on their own. According to Piaget (1952), these schemas are frameworks, also known as memories and perceptions that help children organize and understand information about the world around them. Put simply, schemas can be imagined as file cabinets in a brain full of files representing events in one's life—memories and understandings. New life experiences and active engagement can change the content of the existing files, replace files altogether, or add to the cabinet alongside the existing files. Piaget called this process "The Stages of Cognitive Development" (Piaget, 1952; Maynards & Thomas, 2004).

Russian psychologist Lev Vygotsky also studied children. It fascinated him that young children were born into a world where adults were motivated to help them learn, so while Piaget (1952) claimed a child's knowledge was gained by active engagement with the world around them, Vygotsky (1967) took this further and suggested development arises from social interchange, or a two-way, back-and-forth relationship between a child and their environment, including the adults who educate them (Vygotsky, 1967; Maynards & Thomas, 2004). That is why it is so important to play with children when they are little.

In 1979, scientist James MacGregor Burns, an authority on leadership studies, published a book titled *Leadership*. In his book, he takes the idea of child learning and development and connects it to the potential for children to display leadership qualities. He wrote:

"Children are not mere sponges, soaking up culture and influences…they are generators of ideas…they turn projects into their environment…they are shapes to a large degree; their capacity to learn what is offered, their selectivity, and the way in which they integrate their knowledge…is applied in specific social and political situations" (Burns, 1979, p. 86).

In his work, Burns also stressed the positive and negative influence that children have over each other (1979). This can be seen during play or discussed when kids come home from school, and you ask them how their day went.

In line with this theory, John W. Gardner wrote a book titled *On Leadership (1990)*. In it, Gardner states that leadership does have roots in childhood. He notes that intelligence can be primarily genetic and explains the way in which early childhood experiences of learning language are also leadership-influenced, and that may be on for the reasons why we need to read to our children. According to Gardner, the need for achievement sparks development in the first two years of life, but the desire to learn changes constantly from early school age to early adulthood. Gardener concludes that modeled behavior, behavior standards, and imposed values in the home all affect the later emergence of traits for the development of leadership (1990).

Robert K. Greenleaf (2002) developed "Servant Leadership." He stated that a good leader should not focus on being the most important or powerful figure, but should put the needs of their followers first, underlining the importance of teamwork and embracing one's community. This produces strong, ethical, caring leaders whose followers grow and develop, and makes for a better society. Greenleaf goes on to say that existing education systems have problems. He states that the difficulties with them are

1. *lack of leadership preparation,*
2. *preferential treatment and better leadership opportunities for those from more privileged backgrounds, and*
3. *lack of educational teachings of ethics and moral values*

(Greenleaf, 2002).

Integrating the ideas of active engagement, social learning, and the role of education in creating good leaders, Kouzes and Posner (2007) authored a book titled *The Leadership Challenge*. They believe that if a caring adult plays the role of a teacher, pastor, coach, or community leader, *they* set the example of a good leader for the children. This is because children seek guidance from the people who influence their daily lives on how to respond in competitive situations, handle a crisis, deal with stress and loss, and resolve ethical and moral dilemmas (Kouzes & Posner, 2007).

In this chapter, we have seen not only the theories around the ways children learn to be leaders from active engagement with the world around them, but also the roles that caregivers, educators, and authority figures can play in a child's perception of leadership, encouraging them to be leaders themselves and sparking various leadership qualities. The theories covered are summarized below for easy reference:

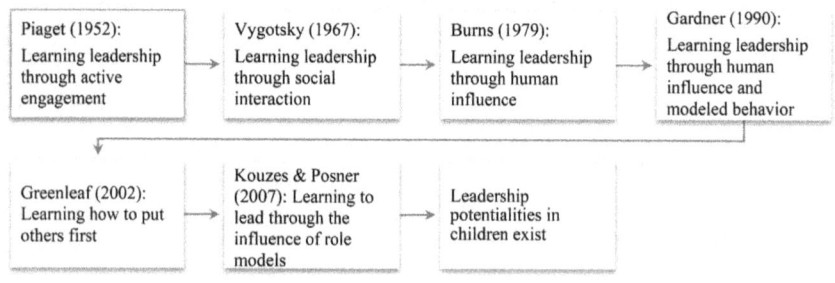

While we have now seen that leadership skills are developed throughout a child's life, the question of where active leaders come from still remains. Is it nature or nurture? While the theories above can explain how a child acquires knowledge (and therefore leadership skills) by nature, how we nurture and encourage these skills must be further explored, as this is an essential component in growing strong leaders. After all, all great leaders were children first.

EARLY LIFE LEADERSHIP REFLECTIONS

1. What do you see when you see children playing?

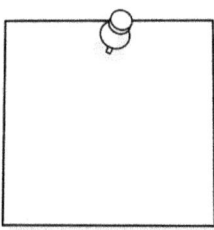

2. How are you nurturing leadership in the children in your life?

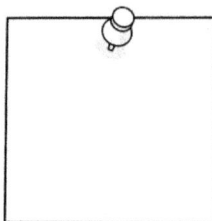

3. Where do you think leaders come from?

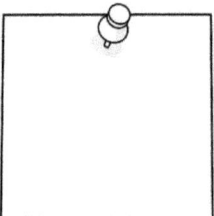

EARLY LIFE LEADERSHIP NOTES

3: Early Life Leadership Research

It is not uncommon to turn on the evening news to a report about youths committing criminal acts ranging from theft to murder. Babies are having babies, preteens and teens are participating in alcohol and drug use, and students are dropping out of schools all over the United States of America. However, young children do not fantasize about becoming "pot-heads" or young parents in the future (Centers for Disease Control and Prevention, 2012). So, where did it all go wrong?

The lack of opportunities for children to practice leadership skills could be a big contributing factor for social problems and hardships of today's youth. This stems from my belief that nurturing a child's leadership abilities at a young age will increase their academic achievement and citizenship positively. My study aims to bring awareness of the fact that *children do have skills and traits* that give them the potential to be leaders and to *emphasize the desperate need for further education on leadership* to equip children with the necessary skills to navigate through their lives and careers in the twenty-first century (Hess, 2010). Additionally, the study also aimed to address the lack of acknowledgment of child leaders, and the fact that data on children and leadership is very limited (Hess, 2010; Rios, 2010; Scharf & Mayseless, 2009).

The *Leadership Skills Checklist* (Castillo, 2001) has nine questions. This study has ten research questions. The nine leadership skills being analyzed are bolded in each of the research questions for the study, which are listed below:

Research Questions

RQ1. Is there a relationship between *personality traits* and **communication** in kindergarten students when controlling for (1) student gender, (2) previous education, and (3) language?

RQ2. Is there a relationship between *personality traits* and **responsibility** in kindergarten students when controlling for (1) student gender, (2) previous education, and (3) language?

RQ3. Is there a relationship between *personality traits* and **encouragement** in kindergarten students when controlling for (1) student gender, (2) previous education, and (3) language?

RQ4. Is there a relationship between *personality traits* and **leadership perception by followers** in kindergarten students when controlling for (1) student gender, (2) previous education, and (3) language?

RQ5. Is there a relationship between *personality traits* and the **ability to delegate to followers** in kindergarten students when controlling for (1) student gender, (2) previous education, and (3) language?

RQ6. Is there a relationship between *personality traits* and *confidence* in kindergarten students when controlling for (1) student gender, (2) previous education, and (3) language?

RQ7. Is there a relationship between *personality traits* and *flexibility* in kindergarten students when controlling for (1) student gender, (2) previous education, and (3) language?

RQ8. Is there a relationship between *personality traits* and *risk-taking* in kindergarten students when controlling for (1) student gender (2) previous education, and (3) language?

RQ9. Is there a relationship between *personality traits* and *dependability* in kindergarten students when controlling for (1) student gender, (2) previous education, and (3) language?

RQ10. Is there a relationship between personality traits and (1) *communication*, (2) *responsibility*, (3) *encouraging others*, (4) *looked up to other students as a "leader,"* (5) *delegates*, (6) *confident*, (7) *flexibility*, (8) *risk-taking*, or (9) *dependability* in kindergarten students when controlling for (1) *student gender*, (2) *previous education*, and (3) *language*?

This list of research questions is the true face of this study, and through this study and my other books, I endeavor to be a voice, an advocate, and a banner in the sky waving the world down, "Hey! Kids are leaders! We need to help them!" But I can't do this alone. Believe in and nurture leadership in the children in your life.

EARLY LIFE LEADERSHIP REFLECTIONS

Reflecting on each leadership skill measured in this study.

1. Why is learning *"**communication skills**"* important for children?

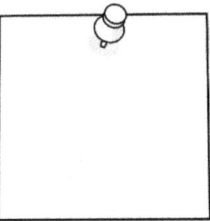

2. Why is learning *"**responsibility**"* important for children?

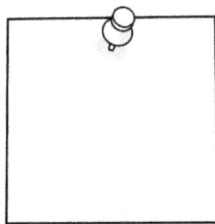

3. Why is *"**encouragement**"* important for children?

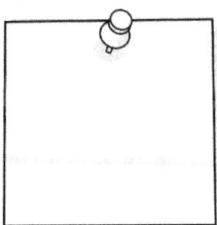

4. Why is being perceived as a **"leader by followers"** important for children?

5. Why is possessing the **"ability to delegate to followers"** important for children?

6. Why is having **"confidence"** important for children?

7. Why is learning **"flexibility"** important for children?

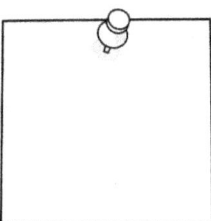

8. Why is learning *"to take risks"* important for children?

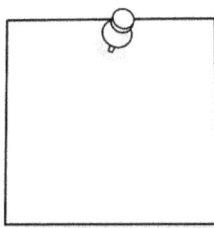

9. Why is learning to be **"dependable"** important for children?

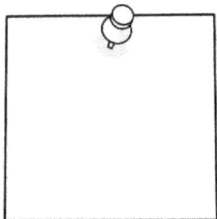

EARLY LIFE LEADERSHIP NOTES

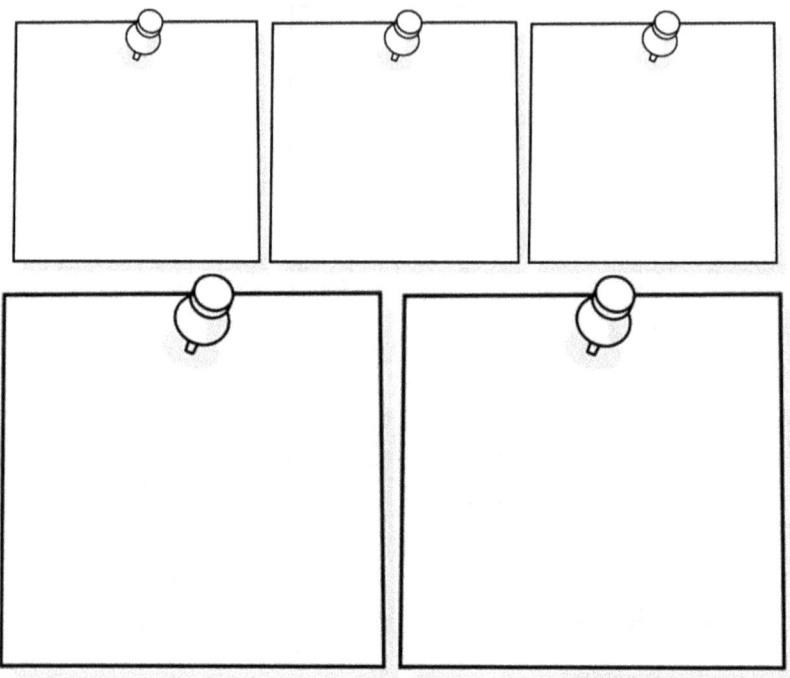

4: What Does Research Say?

In this chapter, we will review literature in the area of children, leadership, and its relationship to personality traits to better establish why certain variables within my study are important. As we have discussed, the heartbeat of my study centers on leadership skills and personality traits in children. Everyone is as different as their fingerprints. There are many things that differentiate us from one another, some seen as early as birth. A mother may experience one baby being needier than another child, or one baby who enjoys being cradled while its sibling does not.

The Great Man Theory

In the 20th century, leadership traits were studied in order to help determine the source of people's greatness. After studying the "Great Man Theory," I started to questions what personality traits make "great men" great. Lord, de Vader, and Alliger (1986) found personality traits were strongly associated with an individual's perception of one's self (Lord, de Vader, & Alliger, 1986). The Great Man Theory is a historical concept that professes great leaders are born, not made. Burns also concedes leadership is something that is embedded within us

(Burns, 1978). According to Warren Bennis (2009), author of *On Becoming a Leader,* some people were lucky enough to be born with the desire, and the ability, to make things happen. For some, the desire to achieve is embedded; but for a lucky few, it's not calculated—it is an innate ability, like breathing. This is important to consider because adults do not always think of children as leaders, and consequently do not provide opportunities for them to lead (Bennis, 2009).

Becoming a Resonant Leader by McKee, Boyatzis, and Johnston (2008) presents the idea that leadership is both innate and developed. According to the authors, one good characteristic of strong leadership is an inherited tendency to be optimistic, though they admit more characteristics of effective leadership can be learned and developed over time. They add that family experiences in early childhood, educational settings, community, and work all shape a child's abilities to build and sustain relationships, to guide, to manage themselves, and to influence others (McKee, Boyatzis, & Johnston, 2008).

Many believe some have a natural-born capacity to lead. Some people seem to have a "certain something" elevating them above the rest of the group that enables them to be what we call "natural-born leaders." Such unique individuals emerge in every situation, and many distinguish themselves at an early age. Perhaps there is a child who "naturally" organizes the lunch break games at school? Such children have no formal leadership training but have the need to step up to lead the other kids. People were often labeled as natural born leaders because they regularly and habitually model inspiring qualities desired by others (Blank, 2001).

Trait Leadership

To better understand traits within people and how they affect leadership, we must look at the Trait Approach. The Trait Approach was part of early efforts to understand successful leadership and identify personal traits (Daft, 2008). It does not establish a code for leadership but instead emphasizes that certain traits have a positive effect on leading, and states that selecting people with certain traits will increase organizational effectiveness (Rogelberg, 2006).

The Trait Approach has several identifiable strengths. The first strength is based on the idea that people feel the need to see their leaders as "gifted" or extraordinary. The second is that it has centuries of backing through research. The third is conceptual in nature, and through the leadership process, it can be applied to individuals at all levels and in all kinds of organizations. Lastly, the Trait Approach gives a baseline of what traits should be sought in leaders (Rogelberg, 2006).

Stogdill (1990) was one of the first to survey and identify leadership traits. He determined that the average individual in a leadership role is different from an average group member when it comes to the following eight traits: intelligence, alertness, insight, responsibility, initiative, persistence, self-confidence, and sociability. This survey also indicated that an individual's leadership traits must be relevant to the situation (Bass & Stogdill, 1990).

Stogdill's (1990) second survey was published in 1974 and validated the idea that a leader's characteristics were indeed a part of leadership. The second survey identified ten characteristic traits in leaders (Bass & Stogdill, 1990):

1. Drive for responsibility and task completion
2. Vigor and persistence in pursuit of goals
3. Risk-taking and originality when problem-solving
4. Drive to exercise initiative in social situations
5. Self-confidence and a sense of personal identity
6. Willingness to accept the consequences from decisions and actions
7. Readiness to absorb interpersonal stress
8. Willingness to tolerate frustration and delay
9. Ability to influence another person's behavior
10. Capacity to structure social interaction systems to the purpose at hand

Additionally, in 1959, a similar study was conducted that resulted in 1,400 findings regarding personality and leadership in small groups. This research suggests that personality traits could distinguish leaders from non-leaders, and identified leaders possessed six common strengths: intelligence, masculinity, adjustment, dominance, extroversion, and conservatism. Bass & Stogdill (1990), in correlation with Lord, (1986), found that intelligence, masculinity, and dominance were significantly related to how leaders were perceived (Bass & Stogdill, 1990).

Kirkpatrick and Locke (1991) believed that leaders differ from non-leaders through six traits: drive, motivation, integrity, confidence, cognitive ability, and task knowledge. According to Bass & Stogdill, individuals can either be born with these traits, or they can learn them, although some leaders benefitted from a combination of both (Bass & Stogdill, 1990).

A summary of the leadership traits uncovered by a few of the studies can be found in the table below:

Stogdill (1948)	Mann (1959)	Stogdill (1974)	Lord, de Vader, and Alliger (1986)	Kirkpatrick (1991)	Zaccaro, Kemp, and Bader (2004)
Intelligence Alertness Insight Responsibility Initiative Persistence Self-Confidence Sociability	Intelligence Masculinity Adjustment Dominance Extroversion Conservation	Achievement Persistence Insight Initiative Self-confidence Responsibility Cooperativeness Tolerance Influence Sociability	Intelligence Masculinity Dominance	Drive Motivation Integrity Confidence Cognitive Ability Task Knowledge	Cognitive Abilities Extroversion Consciousness Emotional Stability Openness Agreeableness Motivation Social Intelligence Self-monitoring Emotional Intelligence Problem Solving

Table 2.1: Studies of Leadership Traits and Characteristics (Northouse, 2010)

The Big Five Personality Traits

Over the past twenty-five years, *The Big Five Personality Traits* have evolved to be the accepted set of basic factors making up a leader's personality. *The Big Five Personality Traits* have been coined as OCEAN by students and researchers, and are openness, consciousness, extroversion, agreeableness, and neuroticism (Goldberg, 1989).

To connect *The Big Five Personality* Traits to the above-identified leadership traits, researchers Judge, Bono, Ilies, and Gerhardt (2002), executed an immense analysis of 78 leadership and personality studies published between 1967 and 1998. They found a significant relationship between *The Big Five Personality Traits* and effective leadership. High degrees of consciousness and openness and a low degree of neuroticism were noted as the most important traits of effective leadership (Goldberg, 1989).

Bass and Avoilo (1994) classified the traits of leaders into clusters: (1) biographical and demographical characteristics, such as age, sex, health, marital status, and job experience, (2) intellectual or cognitive skills, such as knowledge, intelligence and abilities, (3) personality or non-cognitive characteristics, such as interests, motivation, and values. According to their study, these traits affect individual performance, motivation, commitment, involvement, loyalty, and team performance (Bass & Avolio, 1994).

Bass and Avolio state that "natural-born leaders" are selected by their peers because leadership is seen as emergent, and they found that elected leaders possess the trait and qualities necessary to provide direction naturally. Furthermore, they discovered that the characteristics of effective team leaders include (1) knowledge of the group process, (2) the ability to think and react decisively, and (3) the ability to articulate a position clearly (Bass and Avolio, 1994).

In terms of my study, the overview above shows that understanding personality traits and their effects on leadership is key for parents and educators to identify the dominant personality and leadership traits in their children early on. Early identification will help nourish and cultivate future leaders and increase the opportunities for children to participate in leadership experiences.

Leadership in Children

Leadership development enhances a child's "natural abilities" and allows them to access higher levels of leadership ability. The enhancement of specific skills attached to leadership development can help the child progress to greater leadership ability levels and create well-defined effective leadership capacity (Lester, 2002).

One of the biggest misconceptions society has is that children are too young to understand leadership. However, children can develop leadership skills at an early age (Karnes & Bean, 1995). Victoria Ruth Fu (1970) from the University of North Carolina researched children and leadership. Fu titled her thesis *"The Development of a Nursery School Leadership Observation Schedule and a Nursery School Leadership Rating Scale."* The three main objectives were to find a reliable way to (1) develop a valid and reliable instrument for direct recording of leadership behavioral characteristics of nursery school children, (2) develop a valid and reliable scale for teachers to use when rating leadership behavioral characteristics of nursery school children, and (3) determine the correlation between the observational measure of children's leadership behavioral characteristics and the teacher's rating of children's leadership behavior (Fu, 1970).

Fu's (1970) study was conducted by the (1) formulation and definition of the problem of leadership, (2) review of previous literature, and (3) the composition of measurement surveys for small children. Fu (1970) states leadership can be viewed as a social role played by an individual in a given social situation and identified two main types of leadership among children. Type one is "bullying," and type two is "diplomatic." She noted that some children manipulate or threaten other children to overpower them, but contrastingly, others take the lead by inspiring, encouraging, guiding, and cooperating with their peers (Fu, 1970).

Fu (1970) also published a study on the leadership-followership behaviors of 48 kindergarteners. Their socioeconomic backgrounds varied, and they were observed during free play. Each social class was composed of 12 boys and 12 girls, and their ages ranged from 5.5-6.3 years of age. The Nursery School Leadership Observation Schedule (NSLOS) used consisted of four main categories: (1) successful leadership, (2) unsuccessful leadership, (3) followership, (4) non-conforming behavior (Fu, 1979).

The middle-class children had higher followership scores than lower social class children. There was also a significant correlation between the observed successful and unsuccessful leadership in girls, and the significant relationship between unsuccessful leadership and followership among children who were on a lower socioeconomic level. This meant that these children conformed better to accepted rules but were less strong in leading and getting others to follow. Middle-class kindergarteners showed a positive correlation between successful leadership and followership, meaning these children were more successful in both leading well and getting other children to follow (Fu, 1979).

Through observation, the development of leadership in children was identified in four characteristic stages:

1. Determination
2. A better grasp of abstract and social control
3. An increased awareness of personalities
4. A more sufficient memory to pursue remote goals rather than more immediate objectives

The possession and development of these characteristics, which were needed for effective leadership, were directly related to the social ability of the children (Fu, 1979).

By taking one-minute samples of behavior, her observations of spontaneous play in nursery school children showed that the "bully" and "diplomat" distinction between the two types of leaders existed even at the preschool age. It was observed that the "bullying" leader may control a large number of children and employed brute force in "bossing" the small group they chose for their "gang." Furthermore, the likelihood of being part of this "gang" increases with age, as the frequency of independent play decreases as children grow older. There was a trend toward the development of leadership as the school year advanced (Parten, 1933).

Harlie Owens (2007), the founder of the Leadership Institute, published her findings on children and leadership in her book, *Creating Leadership in the Classroom*. She asked teachers, "At what age should leadership be developed?" While 20% of teachers answered that this should be at three to five years of age, 34% of teachers answered five to seven years of age, and 31% of teachers answered eight to eleven years of age, only 10% of teachers answered 12-16 years of age. Fully 85% of teachers believed leadership is a combination of learned and innate behaviors (Owens, 2007).

In the United States, from age five to six, children attend kindergarten. Kindergarteners were difficult to keep focused, but Owens found their curiosity over different adults being present in the room compensated for it, and for the most part, the young children paid attention. In this age group, 90 to 100% of the kids raised their hands when asked a question. However, Owens (2007) found children often put their hands up even if they really didn't understand the question. Their enthusiasm and eagerness to participate in the learning process preceded their knowledge of their answer. Unfortunately, Owens could not scientifically validate this enthusiasm. Despite the results, the researcher was curious and decided to continue with the study. Children were asked why they thought they were leaders, but they were unable to formulate an answer. However, a couple of students did say, "My friend let me." They demonstrated their ability to synthesize the question and provide appropriate answers with concrete examples (Owens, 2007).

Therefore, a teacher's perception is very important. During Owens' study, teachers gave categories in which they felt the leaders in their classes performed strongly, including:

Categorized leadership themes from the teacher's perspective were organized by frequency. Teachers noticed several items: (1) goal/task—being able to realize goals or achieve a required outcome, (2) team/group—control or organize a group, promote teamwork engaging behavior to inspire, motivate or encourage, and (3) people-centered—respect individuals, allow them to achieve their potential, empower others, and understand their needs.

Within those categories, there arose many different perceptions of leadership. Many teachers seemed to view leadership as action-centered, task-oriented and focused on project management, rather than something that considered the values, needs, or interests of group members. The most frequent words used by these teachers to describe leaders were "motivated, inspires a vision, decision making, provided direction, takes control, enables others, listens to others, respects others, communicates, influences, and is a role model" (Owens, 2007). The teacher's perceptions were important because teachers can affirm when children were seen as leaders in the classroom.

During play, one or more leaders emerged within the play setting. Empirical and theoretical studies on young children's leadership play in the classroom can be used as identification of leading and following skills, the skills of effective leader/followers, and types of unskilled leaders which included bullies, isolates, and rascally children. Both leading and following were viewed as essential aspects of effective social participation (Trawick-Smith, 1988), since both leaders and followers were required in everyday settings. After observing the peer interaction that took place in play, teachers examined

1. whether or not children took the lead during group activities,
2. how children looked up to young leaders,
3. if these leaders were listened to,
4. how others listened to the leaders, and
5. whether the leaders helped others

(Owens, 2007).

In addition to observing the dynamics of socialization groups, teachers were asked to be aware of certain skills. In order of frequency, they were

1. whether the child could express their opinions,
2. whether the child had good organizational skills,

3. whether the child was confident,

4. whether the child took responsibility,

5. whether the child stood out,

6. whether the child acted independently

(Owens, 2007).

Owens' research yielded four major conclusions:

Conclusion 1: Everyone has leadership potential. This is limitless and is not dependent on someone's job role or title. In fact, ordinary people can demonstrate leadership potential in their everyday lives (Owens, 2007).

Conclusion 2: No two people express leadership in the same way. Great leaders like Winston Churchill, Mother Teresa, and Nelson Mandela can be admired, studied and remembered as role models for leadership, but can never be exactly replicated as leaders. Everyone must find their own leadership style and learn how to express and communicate that leadership effectively (Owens, 2007).

Conclusion 3: One cannot become a leader overnight. Becoming an effective leader is a lifelong learning process. When learning stops, leadership potential becomes limited (Owens, 2007).

Conclusion 4: To have leadership expressed throughout schools and organizations, a structural change is needed to make them more democratic and less hierarchical. This must be done in such a way for all involved to have a responsibility, as opposed to just a few (Owens, 2007).

Fukada, Fukada, and Hicks (1994), in a study titled "The Relationship Between Leadership and Sociometric Status Among Preschool Children," examined the relationship between leadership behavior and the status of individuals within their social relationships among preschool children in Japan. The leadership behaviors of 24 six-year-old Japanese children were observed during free play. The children were then categorized into three sociometric (or social relationship) status groups. Children who had a high status in their relationships showed greater leadership behavior than those with lower status in their relationships (Fukada, Fukada, & Hicks, 1994).

According to Fukada, Fukada, and Hicks, leadership ability can be learned, measured, and developed. If it is alleged that leadership can be learned, it follows that it can be developed. Once leadership measurement takes place, it should be followed by a plan for the development of leadership skills, making the whole process fundamental in building a strong stable of young leaders for America, as well as the main concern for those interested in educating youth and in equipping them with leadership promise for the future.

Currently, there *are* instruments available to measure leadership ability, but the vast majority of schools have not utilized them, and some have not been consistently updated. One of the most common ways to measure leadership ability is to observe the leadership characteristics of a child in relation to their leadership *capabilities*. Their capabilities can be identified through routine observations that require the child to display characteristics relevant to leadership. Ideally, the observer making such determinations should be someone who has a relationship with the child (Lester, 2002).

The Role of Parents, Educators, and the Classroom

According to Lester (2002), no one knows a child better than their parents, so parents play an essential role in identifying leadership ability and capacity. However, school-age children are not only influenced by their parents but also their peers. Observing students in the classroom is important, for it is where children display their leadership skills.

In an article titled, "Who's the Boss? Young Children's Power and Influence in an Early Childhood Classroom," two researchers conducted classroom observations and teacher interviews to analyze three young children. The children who were considered classroom leaders by their teachers created multifaceted dilemmas for their teachers throughout the school year. Lee and Recchia (2008) evaluated their interactions with teachers and peers. Their findings showed that the leadership of the observed children did have a powerful influence on their peers, which could be both positive and negative, as the children used their influence to provoke and challenge teachers. These findings present an opportunity to address leadership and its influential power in early childhood students, as well as its effect on classroom practices (Lee & Recchia, 2008).

Alexis A. Soffler's (2011) dissertation through the University of Colorado, "What is the Nature of Children's Leadership in Early Childhood Educational Setting?" studied kindergarten students. The study, a grounded theory, described the leadership experiences of four- and five-year-old preschool and kindergarten children in a school atmosphere. Nine children were observed while participating in learning and play, and the study found that leadership came as a result of the skills of an individual child being called for in a particular situation or by other children in a combined preschool and kindergarten program. Using qualitative grounded theory methodology, a theory regarding young children's leadership interactions were constructed. This theory proposes leadership events and roles are a result of the dynamic fit between the individual child, the environmental needs and expectations, and the level of leadership understanding, overlaid by decisions enacted by all members throughout the event (Soffler, 2011).

Soffler's findings suggested that educators should focus on building leadership foundations in early childhood classrooms by exploring different social environments, nurturing diverse skill sets in all children, and by examining decision making when addressing leadership learning with children (Soffler, 2011).

Ryoko Yamaguchi (2001) from the University of Michigan focuses on how motivation influences the emergence of leadership in the classroom. Students were divided into fourth- and fifth-grade classrooms and assigned either a mastery (focus on learning and improving) or performance (focus on social comparison and competition) goal. Groups within these classrooms were set according to gender (majority-female or majority-male) and ability (high-ability, low-ability, or mixed-ability) groups. In the first study, 249 elementary students, nested within 99 groups across 17 classrooms, worked on a collaborative math task for 30 minutes. The Leadership Behavior Descriptor Questionnaire was adapted to create two scales of emergent leadership: task-focused and relationship-focused leadership.

Task-focused leadership was found to be lower in a majority-female group. In terms of relationship-focused leadership, the mastery of boys was lower than girls. While task and relationship-focused leadership were not related to performance in the math task, female-majority, high-ability, and mixed-ability groups performed better (Ryoko, 2001).

In the second study, 90 students from the first study were randomly selected and videotaped. It was found that while positive leadership was higher in female-majority groups who focused on learning, negative leadership was also higher in girls. Task leadership was higher in girls in the female-majority groups, but overall, all classes of leadership resulted in a better performance with the math task. Therefore, we can say that the motivational context of doing well in the math task influences the emergence of leadership and achievement in the classroom (Ryoko, 2001).

Perez, Chassin, Ellington, & Smith (1982) examined classroom leadership in the Early Childhood Cluster, College Learning Laboratory. At the State University College at Buffalo, three early childhood teachers questioned two kindergarten groups of 20 five-year-old (full-day sessions) and two nursery school groups of three- and four-year-old (each in combined-ages half-day sessions). In addition to being observed, the students were privately interviewed: (1) Who's your best friend/favorite friend in the classroom? (2) Who should I (the teacher) choose to help me teach the children? (3) Who would you choose to play within the motored (activity) room?

Through this process, children identified leadership within their group (Perez et al., 1982) and rationalized their choices by explaining "he knows stuff," "she remembers," and "he/she is so good." It was found that the children's commentary matched up with the teachers' observations of classroom leaders. In these observations, attention was directed to three specific factors contributing to leadership that could be encouraged in the classroom:

1. Verbal ability
2. Independence
3. A sense of structure

Observations were focused on these elements, and classroom experiences were designed to nurture the leadership abilities in the classroom (Perez et al., 1982).

Kathryn Jane Karschney (2003) studied leadership in eleven children who had repeated contact and conversations with adults through Gonzaga University. The purpose of this research was to discover how children relate their experiences to leadership and change. Through the children's perceptions of structured intergenerational dialogue, Karschney utilized qualitative research in a multiple-case study method (Karschney, 2003).

Over a two-year period, two or more children attended six different leadership institutes accompanied by the researcher. Data was collected in three ways: participant observations during the leadership institutes, interviews with the children, and written journals kept by the participants. The analysis of this data led to findings presented in two ways: (1) characteristics of each child's experiences, and (2) characteristics of the setting (the leadership institute) which facilitated or inhibited opportunities for dialogue (Karschney, 2003).

Karschney (2003) found that all the participants demonstrated some cognitive ability to deal with one or more adults in the institute. In addition, four essential elements were found to encourage a dialogue with adults and the acquisition of leadership skills through such discourse:

1. The approachability of the adults

2. The willingness of the adults to balance power relations between them and the children

3. The discussions themselves encouraging children to be leaders

4. Opportunities for divergent thinking

(Karschney, 2003)

According to the Minnesota Early Childhood Teacher Educators, Kindergarten Task Force, (1986):

Observers of young children have seen intense and concentrated eagerness to discover and explore their world. The observer notes the development of unique personality characteristics within each child... (Minnesota Early Childhood Teacher Educators, Kindergarten Task Force, 1986)

Linda Rios (2010) is another researcher who has researched leadership behaviors in children and their relationship to academic achievement, success in school, and higher education. The purpose of Rios's study was to establish a connection between leadership behavior in bilingual children and their academic achievement and performance. Rios aimed to make it possible to design leadership programs and curriculums aimed specifically at promoting leadership development within children (Rios, 2010).

The federal No Child Left Behind (NCLB) legislation of 2001 mandated standardized testing. Rios used the standardized Texas Assessment of Knowledge and Skills (TAKS) scores in numerous grades and disciplines to measure the correlation between academic success and leadership, while the state of Texas used the TAKS test to evaluate student achievement in public schools based on the state's curriculum, the Texas Essential Knowledge and Skills (TEKS) (Rios, 2010).

Rios (2010) explained in her dissertation, titled *The Relationship Between Emerging Leadership Behavior in Children and Their Academic Performance*, that children must demonstrate determination, intelligence, integrity, and self-confidence to perform well academically, and as we saw earlier, these are the same skills perceived by adults as leadership skills (Rios, 2010). She stressed that children succeed in school when they feel connected to it, and the risk of dropping out becomes more minimal. When this happens, children gain a significant higher education to develop into contributing adults and possibly the leaders of tomorrow (Rios, 2010).

Evangelina Villagomez (2007) investigated leadership development in disadvantaged or minority young children in a dissertation titled *An Inductive Analysis of the Self-Perceptions of Young Children Related to*

Leadership as a Construct. The research participants in Villagomez's study were children ages 9-12 who were predominantly of Mexican-American descent. These children attended either public or private elementary schools in an urban area of San Antonio, Texas. The data highlighted the importance of values and integrity in servant leadership and found that there was a relationship between gender, location, and the way in which a leader is described (Villagomez, 2007).

Children Led by Children and Learning Leadership

Examining leadership through the perception of children is important because it can help address misconceptions they may have with regard to leadership. It can also help develop curricular activities to enhance leadership characteristics in all children in order to improve their educational completion rates and success (Villagomez, 2007).

Robin Eileen Sacks (2009) completed her dissertation, titled *Natural Born Leaders: An Exploration of Leadership Development in Children and Adolescents,* through the University of Toronto. Sacks aimed to identify fundamental elements of leadership development in children and adolescents using the study which was a multi-phase mixed-methods research in both qualitative and quantitative data collection. Phase one of the data collection included focus groups at eleven schools (six elementary and five secondaries) made up of approximately six to eight students each. Phase two of the data collection was a survey of youth leaders from across Canada (Sacks, 2009) through a documented partnership with "Me to We," a Toronto-based organization aimed at helping teachers and students learn about world issues and take action by fundraising for projects in developing countries as well as offering overseas volunteer opportunities (see www.metowe.org). "Me to We" also offers tips for teachers on how to establish a team of student leaders to carry out service projects, as well as a leadership curriculum.

Interested teachers were given a link to the survey to pass along to their "Me to We" student leaders to complete. The survey was designed to further investigate and quantify the findings that emerged from the focus groups' data analysis.

The focus group samples consisted of student leaders from eleven schools (six elementary and five secondaries). Each school's principal was asked to nominate six to eight student leaders to participate in the focus groups. The nomination form requested that principals nominate student leaders who represented various forms of school involvement and leadership and required them to justify each nomination. Principals were encouraged to consult guidance counselors and lead teachers in making the selections. As a result, the makeup of the student focus groups represented a wide range of abilities, perspectives, and interests (Sacks, 2009).

In elementary school, principals chose student leaders on the basis of their personal qualities, while high school principals selected students on the basis of their involvement in a range of activities. Remarks typical of elementary principals said that pupils were "bright," "responsible," "good listeners," "all-around supportive students," "showing leadership qualities," "popular among peers," "had complex thinking skills," and "showed perseverance." In contrast, the high school nomination forms stated roles, such as members of the student council (presidents and vice presidents), student trustees, prefects, event organizers, team captains, and members of school leadership classes (Sacks, 2009).

The sample for this survey included 164 students from elementary and secondary schools across Canada. Seventy-eight percent of the respondents were girls. Thirty-four percent of respondents were in elementary school, and 66% were in secondary school (Sacks, 2009).

Of the students surveyed, 25.4% believed they were born a leader, compared to 44.8% who believed they developed into a leader. Nearly one-third of students said they "weren't sure." High school students were more likely than elementary school students to believe they were born leaders (29% of high school students compared with 17.1% of elementary students) (Sacks, 2009).

Moreover, 79.9% of students believed that anyone could be a leader, compared to 20.1% who did not believe everyone has it in them to be a leader. That variable also revealed differences between elementary and secondary students, with 88.1% of elementary students saying anyone can be a leader compared to 76.1% of secondary students. For high school students, school requirements and résumé-building played a large role in their decision to get involved with leadership opportunities.

Outside those two factors, elementary and secondary students' responses were nearly identical, with their top three motivators including (1) to help with a cause or issue (66.5%), (2) to be a leader in school or community (59.1%), and (3) to learn leadership skills (55.5%). Other factors included making new friends (43.3%), gaining confidence (42.1%), and following through with a teacher recommendation (28.7%) (Sacks, 2009).

Overall, students reported responsible behavior in both elementary and secondary school. Increased risk-taking was identified in high school students, with significantly more students reporting skipping school. High school students were also more likely than elementary school students to engage in political conversations, and to volunteer (Sacks, 2009).

When participants were questioned about who their top role models for leadership were, students listed a variety of people, ranging from those they had close personal relationships with, celebrities, and political figures. Elementary school students listed celebrities such as Britney Spears, Angelina Jolie, Tyra Banks, the Dixie Chicks, John Lennon, Dr. Phil, Bono, and Wayne Gretzky. They also mentioned activists such as Nelson Mandela, Craig Keilburger, Irshad Manji, Terry Fox, David Suzuki, Justin Trudeau, Jane Goodall, and Rosa Parks. All students listed these along with people close to them, like teachers and parents. Secondary school students listed celebrities like Oprah, Ellen Degeneres, various athletes, and activists Craig Keilburger and Al Gore. Concurrent to elementary students, secondary students also listed people known to them, such as their parents, bosses, coaches, church leaders, older siblings, older players on the football team at school, grandparents, and their teachers (Sacks, 2009).

Student participants were also given a variety of leadership traits and asked to rate their importance. There were no significant differences between elementary and secondary student responses. The beliefs about which traits constitute "a good leader" were also surveyed, and these traits were (1) passion, (2) honesty, and (3) "easy to talk to." The top three leadership behaviors noted were

1. motivating others to make things happen,
2. always trying to help out, and
3. making sure everyone in the group feels included (Sacks, 2009).

Sacks stated that students in the focus group seemed most engaged when discussing their emerging leadership identities. Most had not had the opportunity to reflect on their personal growth and the elements contributing to their confidence as a leader. Along with their apparent understanding of what makes a good leader, students were able to perceive and wanted to develop leadership behavior and traits within themselves.

Deborah Lee Fox (2012), another researcher of leadership in children, completed her dissertation from the University of New Orleans. Her research was titled *Teachers' Perceptions of Leadership in Young Children* and aimed to explore how teachers described, recognized, and could potentially influence leadership behaviors in children ranging from four to six years old. She intended to answer three research questions:

1. How do teachers describe leadership in young children?

2. Given scenarios, do teachers recognize leadership behaviors in young children?

3. Given scenarios, how do teachers believe they might influence (support or discourage) leadership behavior in young children?

The first and third questions were analyzed based on open-ended responses from teachers. The second question was answered through the survey of 133 early childhood teachers and teachers of the gifted with the *Recognizing Leadership in Children Survey* (RLIC). This evaluated the teacher's recognition of leadership through classroom scenarios in actual classroom observations (Fox, 2012).

Of the 133 participants, 98% were female, with 1.5% male participants. The independent variables in this study were teaching experience and the educational level of teachers (degrees and certifications). The dependent variables in this study were a child's leadership behavior and their multifaceted characteristics (Fox, 2013).

Fox's study indicates that teachers described child leaders as helpful, self-confident, and good communicators. Teachers recognized overt child leadership behaviors more often than subtle ones, and when they did recognize that certain behaviors were associated with leadership, they were more likely to encourage that behavior. When teachers did not recognize leadership in the child's behavior, they tended to respond in a discouraging manner.

Therefore, Fox theorized that if teachers learned to recognize child leadership, they could be supportive, and create more developmentally-appropriate, early childhood classrooms. This reinforces the belief that leadership can be learned in educational environments through activities that promote developmentally-appropriate leadership practices. Three-, four-, and five-year-olds, in particular, *must* experience concrete learning activities within the context of their everyday lives to learn abstract constructs such as leadership (Shipley, 1998; Fox, 2012).

Lisa Cornelison Bohlin (2000) from Indiana University titled her dissertation *Determinants of Young Children's Leadership During Play*. Bohlin's premise was that a child's power to influence emerges during infancy, and that influence could be used in leadership with peers as the child grows older. In this study, Bohlin noted three levels of variables that could influence her findings: (1) individual—the child's age, gender, temperament, and language development, (2) family—the child's birth order and number of siblings, and (3) peer group—the amount of experience the child had with peers in daycare (Bohlin, 2000).

Bohlin studied 43 six-year-old participants recruited from two nationally accredited childcare facilities. Data used included parents' ratings of child temperaments, an audiotaped sample of their productive speech during play, teacher ratings of their social and communicative ability in the classroom, and demographic information. Each child was paired up with a same-sex peer, and the researcher videotaped the pair's interactions. Observed interactions included helping behaviors, organizational leadership skills, and imitation by their peers, physical aggression, and verbal aggression. In general, children displayed pro-social and organizational leadership more often than physical or verbal dominance when playing with their peers, though older preschoolers used more physical and verbal aggression than younger preschoolers and displayed more examples of organizational leadership during play (Bohlin, 2000).

The only difference in interaction strategies based on gender was that girls used more pro-social strategies and organizational leadership than boys. At all ages, children's temperaments, language development, and months spent with peers predicted the types of strategies they used when trying to influence their peers during play. This indicated that in knowing the child's age, gender, temperament, level of language development, and time spent in childcare, one could predict the profile of peer interaction strategies the child would use with 76.7% accuracy. It is this kind of information that could allow us to develop tailored strategies for leadership education in classrooms.

Carolyn Trevino Castillo (2001) completed her dissertation through Our Lady of the Lake University. It was titled *The Effects of a Dual-language Education Program on Student Achievement and Development of Leadership Abilities*. She studied three schools in Trevino Independent School District for the relationship between a dual language education program and the development of leadership abilities in young children (Castillo, 2001).

Castillo (2001) studied 96 students from kindergarten to second grade (aged five to eight) who participated in the dual language program, and five students who participated in a single language program. Castillo coined and used the *Leadership Skills Checklist* to investigate and identify the impact of the dual language program on the development of children. Interestingly, the dual language participants scored the same as the non-dual language participants on the *Leadership Skills Checklist*, and native English speakers and native Spanish speakers in the dual language program scored equally, suggesting that leadership ability faces no language or environmental barriers.

In the public education system, gifted and talented programs consistently integrate leadership. According to the National Society for the Gifted and Talented, identification of gifted and talented students occurs primarily in an educational setting. School districts organize and execute curriculum-based instruction tailored for the gifted students. Services vary according to the district, but all school districts compile and examine a student's ability, achievement, class grades, standardized scores, IQ, creative and critical thinking, and fine arts accomplishments, often doing so together in a student portfolio (National Society for the Gifted and Talented, 2012).

Leadership is integrated into the Department of Education's definition of "gifted and talented" along with cognitive ability, creative ability, and ability in the visual and performing arts. However, most states have chosen not to identify students as gifted within the area of leadership, claiming it to be too difficult to provide services to develop in an educational setting (Lester, 2002). This researcher disagrees, and this study aims to prove differently.

With growing evidence indicating that leadership capacity is lacking in America's youth, an increased interest in leadership development has emerged in recent years. Leadership is increasingly included in gifted and talented programs, and educators are in the process of developing identification measures and methods to help children build their leadership capacity. Recently, the state of Kentucky launched a statewide effort to serve children better in the area of leadership in the classroom (Lester, 2002).

The National Society for the Gifted and Talented (2012) identifies gifted children as perfectionistic, creative, and idealistic. The gifted and talented umbrella covers six areas: (1) creative thinking, (2) general and intellectual ability, (3) specific academic ability, (4) psychomotor abilities, (5) visual/performing arts abilities, and (6) leadership abilities (National Society for the Gifted and Talented, 2012).

In 1989, *Gifted Child Today* published the article, *Parent's View on Leadership,* written by Suzanne Meriweather and Frances A. Karnes (1989). Seventy-three parents of gifted children across 15 different states were surveyed to examine their perceptions of the development of leadership. Parents identified leader characteristics; their children's strongest and weakest leadership skills; methods for encouraging leadership development; school opportunities for leadership experiences; and the role of teachers, community, and religious organizations (Meriweather and Karnes, 1989).

Miri Scharf and Ofra Mayseless at the University of Haifa published an article, "Socio-emotional Characteristics of Elementary School Children Identified as Exhibiting Social Leadership Qualities." In this article, teachers recognized characteristics in four major socio-emotional domains related to children's social leadership: (1) self-perception, (2) social anxiety, (3) attachment orientation with peers, and (4) interpersonal goals and skills in close friendships (Scharf and Mayseless, 2009).

The study involved 260 fourth- and fifth-grade students (126 boys, 134 girls) from ten classes in a school located in northern Israel. Scharf and Mayseless (2009) concluded that social leadership skills were related to positive self-perceptions in various domains, such as a low level of social anxiety, secure orientation to peers, higher levels of relationship-maintenance goals, lower levels of revenge goals in close friendships, and lower levels of strategy to solve conflicts with friends. Positive self-concept and attachment security were indirectly associated with leadership qualities through their significant association with good social skills (Scharf and Mayseless, 2009).

Charlesworth (1987) agreed, documenting the importance of sociocultural factors and influences during child development, and how they mold children to adulthood (Charlesworth, 1987). These findings reflect an internalization of a positive model of self and others in children who exhibit social leadership qualities (Scharf and Mayseless, 2009).

Nelson (2010), through the University of San Diego, studied leadership aptitude via the Social Influence Survey (SIS). The SIS is a twenty-five-question multiple-choice survey. The study concluded that students who had a higher score on the SIS enjoyed and retained their leadership training and activities. Children who displayed leadership aptitude were sufficiently developed by the age of ten to learn many of the sophisticated social skills required in leadership such as team building, problem-solving, and conflict resolution (Nelson, 2010).

French, Wass, Stright, and Baker (1986) observed decision-reaching behavior of children in same and mixed-age triads to examine leadership behavior patterns. Two hundred and eighty-five children were apportioned to same-sex, same-age groups (seven- eight- or nine-years-old) or same-sex, mixed-age groups (seven-to-nine-years-old). After each group member had individually organized eight pictures by preference, the triads were videotaped as they arrived at a consensus ranking. All verbalizations made in this process were grouped into organizational and procedural comments, statements, and solicitations of preference, following the decisions of others, and off-task behavior (French et al., 1986).

The results of the study in the mixed-age triads comprised of seven-to-nine-year-olds showed heightened organizational behavior and solicitations of opinion in the older group members. However, they exhibited less opinion-giving than their counterparts in the same age groups. Therefore, mixed-age peer experiences may contribute to the acquisition and practice of leadership behavior (French et al., 1986).

Emergent leadership in children was examined in twelve discussion groups in four fourth-grade classrooms. Children's leadership moves were drawn from transcripts of ten free-flowing, open-format discussions of each of the twelve groups. The participants included four teachers, thirty boys, and forty-one girls. The transcripts encompassed 26,000 turns for speaking, including 22,000 child turns, of which 1,700 were judged to serve one of five leadership functions: turn management, argument development, planning and organizing, topic control, and acknowledgment (Li, Anderson, Nguyen-Jahiel, Dong, Archodidou, Kim and Miller, 2007).

The number and type of leadership moves made by the children showed one primary child leader emerged in six out of the twelve children, and in all but one of the remaining groups, leadership was among several children. Even in groups with a dominant leader, leadership functions were widely distributed among group members.

The frequency of leadership moves increased with the progression of the discussions, suggesting emerging leaders were learning how to lead. Girls who received instruction were frequently nominated by their peers as having good ideas, seldom nominated as being too quiet, and exhibited more leadership characteristic than other children (Li et al., 2007).

Non-academic classes such as physical education have historically shown leadership can be infused into children. Through them, teachers and other professionals can offer leadership opportunities in a variety of ways. A study conducted by Lieberman, Arndt, and Daggett (2007) states that leadership experience can improve a student's self-esteem, self-confidence, and self-perception. They argue that it is important for all students, including those with disabilities, to have leadership experience, so a natural extension of inclusion should increase opportunities for leadership and the development of leadership skills (Lieberman, Arndt, & Daggett, 2007).

The studies discussed above all recognize leadership potential in children through real-life examples, social interaction, and learning, and their positive benefits, such as better academic performance, social standing, peer-to-peer interactions, and self-perception.

Personality Traits in Children

It is often questioned what enables successful leaders to be effective. Despite the great diversity among leaders, there are some common personality traits that make effective leaders effective. Very few leaders have entirely leadership-based traits, but in the ones that do, they are well-developed (Campbell, 2007).

Various personality traits remain the same from childhood to adulthood. For example, military, religious, and political leaders are frequently found to have leadership traits and behavior that is above normal throughout their lives. Some of these traits include the desire to excel, intelligence, insight, self-esteem, and forcefulness (Bass & Stogdill, 1990). The personality factors that play an important role in academic success have been studied for a long time. Teacher ratings on the personality and ability of 485 eleven-year-old children were obtained by James Rushton (1966) at the University of Manchester. The Children's Personality Questionnaire (CPQ) was used to document the relationship between these personality characteristics and school success (Rushton, 1966).

When tested on extravert children, the CPQ data showed that emotional maturity assists them in academic pursuits, more relaxed children tend to be better at English, and perseverance is positively related to success in school at this age. Additionally, teachers tended to rate children who were more easy-going as more suitable for academia, more dominant children tended to be more proficient at arithmetic, and the "happy-go-lucky" children appeared to be more likely to benefit from an academic secondary education. The personality questionnaire results and the personality ratings made by teachers concluded that internally-restrained children were more persistent and that children with better self-control have better school records from teachers (Rushton, 1966).

Panyda's study, titled "Personality and Locus of Control among School Children," examined personality alone. The main purpose of this investigation was to find out the differences in personality traits and the Locus of Control among school children, categorizing them by gender. The Locus of Control refers to the extent to which individuals believe they can control events affecting them (Rotter, 1954). A total of sixty children (thirty boys and thirty girls) were taken as a sample. The Children's Personality Questionnaire was used, and a t-test was applied to examine the significant difference between personality and the Locus of Control in children. Results revealed a significant difference in the presence of fourteen personality factors, but no difference in the Locus of Control of either boys or girls (Pandya, 2013).

Professor Rex Campbell at the University of Missouri researched these fourteen traits for his book, *Leadership: Getting It Done*. The fourteen personality traits were personality, persuasiveness, persistence, patience, perceptiveness, probity, praise-giving, positive orientation, people-based, possibilities, practical, progressive, and power-building. Campbell noted that some of these personality traits were learned early in childhood, and others later in life (Campbell, 2007).

Markey, Markey, and Tonsley (2004) examined relations between the ratings of children's personalities using the Five-Factor Model (FFM) of personality and behaviors exhibited by ninety-four children during a videotaped interaction with their parents. Sixty-four different social behaviors were identified, and mothers completed a survey rating their children's personalities (Markey, Markey, & Tonsley, 2004).

The results indicated a pattern of relationships between children's personalities and their behaviors. Their behaviors were related to the traits of neuroticism, extraversion, agreeableness, and conscientiousness. Children rated as neurotic, for example, tended to be self-critical, expressed guilt, manifested self-pity, were insecure, and showed physical signs of tension.

It was found that conscientious children behave like conscientious adults; they seek and provide advice, and exhibit social skills, intelligence, and ambition. Thus, the findings may not only show how behaviors manifest in children but also help to bridge the gap between developmental psychologists' notions of temperaments and personality psychologists' conception of traits. A better understanding of youths' personalities may prove extremely valuable in understanding not only their tendencies to be leaders and followers but their academic strengths and performance (Markey, Markey & Tonsley, 2004).

Through Our Lady of the Lake University, Lucinda Parmer (2012) studied personality traits and leadership in adolescents. Parmer used the Mini-International Personality Item Pool (McCrae & Costa, 1987) instrument and the Roets Rating Scale for Leadership (Roets, 1997) instrument to measure the Big Five Personality Traits within her sample, including conscientiousness, agreeableness, neuroticism, openness to new experiences, and extraversion (Parmer, 2012).

The sample for this study consisted of five groups in public and private sectors from the greater Gulf Coast area. The groups included Galena Park High (Galena Park, Texas), St. Pius X High School (Houston, Texas), Girl Scouts Troops (Houston, Texas), Houston Mayor's Youth Council, and Friends in Family (Alabama/Florida). The total sample involved 264 adolescents (Parmer, 2012).

Parmer (2012) found that the higher the number of clubs and organizations an adolescent belonged to, the stronger their leadership behaviors and extraversion were. Additionally, charismatic leadership predicted the personality dimensions of conscientiousness, agreeableness, and openness to new experiences.

Theodore and Moffitt (2003) observed 1,000 three-year-old children who exhibited five temperament types: under-controlled, inhibited, confident, reserved, and well-adjusted. Twenty-three years later, Theodore and Moffitt reexamined 96% of the children as adults, using multiple methods of comprehensive personality assessment. Their data provides the strongest evidence to date about how children's early-emerging behaviors can foretell their behaviors, thoughts, and feelings as adults, affirming that examining the foundation of the human personality in the early years of life is important (Caspi, Harrington, Milne, Amell, Theodore & Moffitt, 2003).

During the next few years, study members nominated someone who knew them well enough to be an "informant." The informants were mailed questionnaires asking them to describe the study members using a brief version of *The Big Five Inventory* to assess individual differences on the five-factor model of personality: extraversion ("makes things exciting") agreeableness ("cold and distant with others"), conscientiousness ("works until a thing is done"), emotional stability ("is relaxed, handles stress well"), and openness to experience ("likes to reflect and play with ideas"). Informant data was obtained for 946 of the 980 study members who participated in the age 26 assessment. Most informants were best friends, partners, or other family members (Caspi et al., 2003).

From their observations and the observations of the informants, the researchers were able to assess each participant for the presence of the following:

1. Alienation: A high score on the MPQ scale (Multidimensional Personality Questionnaire) indicates a propensity to view the world malevolently. High scorers believe themselves victims of bad luck, and that others wish them harm. They often feel mistreated, deceived, and betrayed by others and by life's circumstances. The under-controlled children scored highest on this scale (Caspi et al., 2003).

2. Stress Reaction: A high score on the MPQ scale indicates a tendency to experience frequent and intense negative emotional

states such as anxiety, distress, and anger. Well-adjusted children scored lowest on this scale and were most likely to overcome upsetting experiences quickly. The under-controlled children scored highest on this scale and acknowledged they often responded with strong negative emotional reactions to many ordinary circumstances (Caspi et al., 2003).

3. Traditionalism: A high score on this MPQ scale indicates conventional, moralistic, and authoritarian beliefs and attitudes. High scorers endorsed strict child-rearing practices, were intolerant, and restricted freedom of expression. The under-controlled children scored highest on this scale in adulthood, whereas the confident children scored the lowest and grew up to be the least conventional adults, with relatively minimal concern for what is "proper" (Caspi et al., 2003).

4. Harm Avoidance: A high score on this MPQ scale indicates a tendency to shun physically dangerous and thrilling experiences. These children preferred safe and mundane activities that posed minimal risk of injury. The inhibited children scored highest on this scale, followed by the more reserved children. Both groups diverged emphatically from the under-controlled children, and, to a lesser extent, the confident children, who as adults said they enjoyed dangerous and exciting experiences and activities (Caspi et al., 2003).

5. Social Potency: A high score on the MPQ scale indicates a propensity for forcefulness and decisiveness. Inhibited and reserved groups of children scored lowest on this scale and preferred that others take charge, for they did not enjoy being the center of attention. Confident children scored significantly higher than every other group of children on this scale, and as adults, they easily assumed leadership roles. The confident leaders described themselves as vigorous, forceful, and dynamic (Caspi et al., 2003).

6. Achievement: A high score on this MPQ scale indicates a tendency toward hard work and determination. The inhibited and reserved groups scored lowest on this scale, suggesting they avoid very demanding projects and are not very ambitious.

In addition to these significant differences, several other trends occurred. The confident and under-controlled children had personality ratings that continued to increase, or at least retain their strength, into adulthood. This not only shows the importance of confidence and room to grow and face challenges while growing up to become leaders but also how the differences between groups of children could be harnessed to design parent-training programs and school-based interventions to improve child development (Caspi et al., 2003).

Similarly, Hampson and Goldberg (2006) investigated the relations between the presence of childhood *Big Five Personality Traits* assessed by elementary-school teachers and similar traits assessed 40 years later by self-reports at midlife. The analyses were based on a relatively large and culturally diverse sample assessed between 1959 and 1967, when the participants were children in Hawaii. The study linked childhood classroom disruptiveness (e.g., restlessness, carelessness with others' property, and being fidgety, impulsive, and irresponsible) with undependability (e.g., being irresponsible and impulsive versus conscientious and neat in appearance). Additionally, childhood extraversion traits (e.g., being outspoken, socially confident, verbally fluent, and assertive) were linked to some adult extraversion counterparts (e.g., being verbally fluent, gregarious, outspoken, and assertive) (Hampson & Goldberg, 2006).

If we continue to explore *The Big Five Personality Traits*, we find that openness has been shown to have a positive correlation with standardized measures of knowledge and achievement and is modestly linked to cognitive ability. Of the Big Five, it has the highest correlations with the SAT® verbal score, but not with math scores. In addition, conscientiousness has consistently predicted academic achievement from preschool through high school, as this has been found to be linked to achievement-striving, self-discipline, diligence, and achievement via independence (Educational Testing Service, 2012).

In general, there does not seem to be a relationship between extraversion and college performance. Before the ages of 11 and 12, extraverted children outperform introverted children; however, among adolescents and adults, some research has shown higher achievement in introverts than extraverts. This change has been attributed to the move from the sociable, less competitive atmosphere of primary school to the rather formal atmospheres of secondary school and higher education where introverted behaviors such as avoidance of intensive socializing become advantageous (Educational Testing Service, 2012).

The study found that agreeable people were often high-performing individuals due to their willingness to adapt and understand their environment. Agreeableness has been shown to predict performance in interpersonal jobs and is an important predictor in a child's tendency to help others. Neuroticism was shown to predict poor academic performance among school-age children. For example, a study of 3,000 13-year-olds proved that emotional stability was related to academic success (Educational Testing Service, 2012).

These studies not only demonstrate the validity of using the traits of neuroticism, openness, extraversion, agreeableness, and conscientiousness to describe children's personalities, but also provide empirical evidence demonstrating that our ideas about the relationship between personalities and behaviors tend to be correct (Markey, Markey & Tinsley, 2004).

Children & Previous Formal Schooling

My research controls for previous formal schooling because quality education programs such as private preschools and pre-kindergarten were found to be important programs for all children, regardless of their background, as they offer communication and socialization (Shipley, 1998).

The New Jersey Department of Education (1996) lists ten signs of a quality program:

1. Children play and work with materials
2. Children have access to various activities
3. Teachers implement small group instruction
4. Classrooms are decorated with student drawings and phonetic spelling examples
5. Children are taught through daily experiences
6. Students work on projects, and worksheets are not a primary activity
7. Children play outside every day
8. Teachers read books to students throughout the day
9. The curriculum is modified for fast and slow learners
10. Children and parents trust and feel a sense of safety about their school

(The New Jersey Department of Education, 1996).

The effects of programs on children's skills are related to their overall quality. Quality is dependent on the experiences children have within classrooms on a day-to-day basis. In order for every child to reach his or her full potential in the classroom, they each must have high-quality, developmentally appropriate instruction, with systems to support the development and learning of children who may be struggling. Researchers have found that although kindergarten reading and math scores were higher for children who had participated in some sort of academic-based care the year prior to enrollment in kindergarten, the largest benefits were found in those children attending state-funded prekindergarten programs (Ackerman & Barnett, 2005).

The Evansville-Vanderburgh School Corporation of Indiana (1980) implemented and conducted a full-day kindergarten pilot program to compare the growth in cognitive, psychomotor, affective (attitude based), and linguistic skills in children who attended the full program with those who did not, only attending for a half-day. Children who received instruction for a full day demonstrated higher abilities and academic growth (Humphrey, Evansville-Vanderburgh School Corp., 1980).

The National Center for Early Development & Learning is a national early childhood research project supported by the U.S. Department of Education's Institute of Education Sciences (IES), formerly the Office of Educational Research and Improvement (OERI). The center conducted research to predict child outcomes at the end of kindergarten from the quality of pre-kindergarten teacher-child interactions and instruction that occurred, in an effort to enhance the cognitive, social, and emotional development of the child receiving instruction. One of the goals of this study was to determine the state of the nation and conduct research on critical issues in early childhood practices (Burchinal, Howes, Pianta, Bryant, Early, Clifford & Barbarin, 2008).

Ultimately, the findings stated that *quality of instruction* makes a child successful in kindergarten, *not* a child's previous formal schooling (Burchinal et al., 2008). Additionally, some further research found both at-risk and not at-risk students to be performing at similar levels in pre-academic skills (Lamon, 2005).

Although short-term research presents results in support of full-day kindergarten, the results were limited and mixed with regard to long-term impacts (Schoenfeldt, 2012).

Gender and Leadership

For decades, what was largely understood of leadership has been based on research conducted by primarily Caucasian men in the United States. In this study, it is important to understand how leadership dynamics are related to gender stereotypes and expectations, interactions between genders, and any impact gender may have on a child's power or status in a particular group (Ayman & Korabik, 2010).

Specific stereotypes attach themselves to a certain gender, although these stereotypes differ according to culture and age. For example, some families encourage young girls to become strong and assertive, while others encourage them to be more submissive. In the classroom, children were often expected to behave and follow classroom rules, though unfortunately, some are labeled as "problem" children. Stereotypically, boys have more behavior problems, whereas girls are expected to be better readers and better-mannered (MacLure, Jones, Holmes & MacRae, 2012).

A large study in New Zealand confirmed gender differences in leadership styles, defining girls' leadership style as directorial and boys' leadership style as dictatorial (Mawson, 2011). If we fast-forward to adulthood, there is empirical research showing that women leaders rated higher as Transformational Leaders than their male colleagues ($p < .01$). At the same time, female leaders scored higher on the "Contingent Reward" than male leaders. On the other hand, male leaders scored higher on the subscales of "Management by Exception-Active" ($p < .05$) and "Management by Exception-Passive" (Eagly, Johannesen-Schmidh & van Engen, 2003). However, some research states there were no significant differences between charismatic behaviors and traits in individual genders (Serafin, 1992).

Brenner's dissertation, titled *Leadership Characteristics in Young Children as Perceived by Caregivers in a Childhood Setting,"* found that while 58% of the classroom population were male, only 42% were identified as classroom leaders. Girls made up 58% of classroom leaders (Brenner, 1991).

Furthermore, the Yamaguchi (2001) study, "The Effects of Achievement Goal Orientation on Emergent Leadership in Children's Collaborative Learning Groups," found that the majority of girls in the study exhibited more leadership behaviors by asking more questions and leading social interaction toward the boys, though they also showed lower individual achievement and tended to shy away from formal leadership roles. In majority groups, boys tended to ignore the girls and show higher individual achievement (Yamaguchi, 2001).

Interestingly enough, in other studies, children gave stereotypical illustrations of leadership. For example, boys said that leaders were "soldiers" or "footballers," while girls would say "the Queen" or "my sister." On the *Leadership Skills Checklist*, an independent t-test for leadership and gender revealed that males had significantly lower leadership scores than females. As Dhuey and Lipscomb noted in their research, non-stereotypical leadership emergence also occurs. For example, in educational settings, girls were seen as emerging leaders in sports (Dhuey and Lipscomb, 2006). Parallel to Dhuey and Lipscomb, it was also found that preschool and kindergarten age girls have leadership traits. Girls have been known to learn how to blend in, so boys are sometimes incorrectly seen as more extraverted leaders (Silverman, 2000). As gender is a part of the leader identification process for young children (Owens, 2007, it was controlled within this study to better document its effects.

Christina DeMara

Bilingual Children & Leadership

Children are all different. There are three basic reasons for these differences: (1) differences in the children themselves, (2) differences in their environments, and (3) opportunities provided for learning. Factors such as personality, learning style, and general learning ability are included within these. Just as people differ in their general ability to master new skills or ideas, children can differ in their general ability to learn a second language, or at least in the speed at which they are able to do so (Wells, 1986).

If the language factor is not controlled for in a study, a disservice is done to English Language Learners (ELL). ELL students have diverse backgrounds, language skills, and educational profiles. Some students can read and write above the average level for their age in their own language, and others have had negative educational experiences that have crushed their motivation. If the stereotypes facing non-native English speakers are taken away, all that is known is some students come from middle-class families with high levels of literacy, while others come from low levels of literacy and extreme poverty (Short & Echevarria, 2005).

A growing number of students in U.S. schools come from non-English homes where the language background is something other than English. English Language Learners are mainly from families with low socioeconomic status and limited educational backgrounds. Thirty years ago, non-English-speaking students were completely submerged into a "sink-or-swim" English environment that did not pay particular attention to their linguistic background (The National Academies Press, 1998). Since then, school districts in the United States have made English Language Learners a priority, as language barriers can cause ELL students to have academic problems. Different approaches have been developed to help increase student development in English.

Cummins (2000) explains that students who can successfully master two languages are more likely to achieve academic success than children who have mastered one language. Cummins makes the distinction between two different kinds of language proficiency, coined as BICS and CALPS. BICS stands for Basic Interpersonal Communication Skills (BICS) and means students are in possession of the "surface" skills of listening and speaking often used in social settings. On the other hand, Cognitive Academic Language Proficiency (CALP) is the basis for a child's ability to use language to keep up with the academic demands placed upon them. According to Cummins (2000), while many children develop native-speaking fluency (i.e., BICS) within two years of immersion in the target language, it takes five to seven years for a child to work on a proficient level comparable to that of native speakers, i.e., CALP (Cummins, 2000).

In some regions of the world, most notably the United States, children have the opportunity to be educated partially through their native language and partially through English, the majority language of the country's dominant society. This dual language education is commonly known as a bilingual education (Genesee & Paradis, 2004). In the state of Texas, during the first term a child is registered for school, their parent or guardian is asked to fill out a "Home Language Survey." Parents disclose what language is predominantly spoken in the home; based on their responses, the child may be placed in an English, Spanish, or bilingual classroom.

In "The Effects of a Dual-language Education Program on Student Achievement and Development of Leadership Abilities" (2001), Castillo found that dual language participants scored the same as the non-dual language participants on the *Leadership Skills Checklist*, but if we look at language and gender, native English-speaking females score one point higher than native Spanish-speaking females. Native Spanish-speaking males score one point higher than native English-speaking males (Castillo, 2001).

In this study, I will be controlling for language because the population used is predominantly Hispanic (Texas English Language Learners Portal, 2012). Acknowledging a student's language demonstrates a "cultural sensitivity" and respect for traditional cultural and linguistic patterns as students welcome those who embrace their culture and the language, no matter what nationality they are (Irby & Lara-Alecio, 1996).

Diverse educational practices and learning opportunities offer higher academic performance among culturally- and linguistically-diverse students (Texas English Language Learners Portal, 2012). Achievement can be obtained through fostering social and emotional support and connections between students, communities, and schools. To do so, teachers and leaders *must* recognize how their own race, childhood, life experiences, and beliefs about culturally-diverse populations influence their commitment to building bridges between school and home (Honigsfeld & Cohan, 2012).

Leadership in children is severely limited when examining Hispanic children. I wanted to be culturally sensitive to the Hispanic population. Cultural sensitivity consists of (1) pride in one's own language and/or culture and respect for traditional cultural and linguistic patterns; (2) a value for oral tradition and history of the native culture; and (3) the suggestion students welcome those who have an openness toward those who embrace their culture and the language, no matter what nationality (Irby & Lara-Alecio, 1996).

Adults seek political leadership in advocates who can give voice to such issues as a livable wage, strong and accessible career paths, and the impact of the quality of life on children's futures. From our neighborhoods and communities, the call for leaders is heard. Only through research and education can the needs for social change and strong leadership flourish. We need to recognize that the essential role of families and communities in successfully raising children to be ethical leaders must be addressed (Sullivan, 2010). Carolyn Castillo completed her dissertation *The Effects of a Dual-language Education Program on Student Achievement and Development of Leadership Abilities*

(2001). Castillo found that dual language participants scored the same as non-dual language participants on the *Leadership Skills Checklist*. The analysis of variances yielded no statistically significant findings on the checklist. But if we look at language and gender on the *Leadership Skills Checklist* instrument, native English-speaking females scored one point higher than native Spanish-speaking females. Native Spanish-speaking males scored one point higher than native English-speaking males (Castillo, 2001).

By analyzing the research and data collected by others, we can better build on the existing body of knowledge. We can see throughout the studies that the ability children have to demonstrate leadership behaviors have been underestimated, and information on children with regard to leadership is limited. As we have discussed, further exploration will facilitate the development of a leadership curriculum and activities for children to help mold them into better students, citizens, and leaders.

EARLY LIFE LEADERSHIP REFLECTIONS

What are three new things you learned in chapter four?

1.

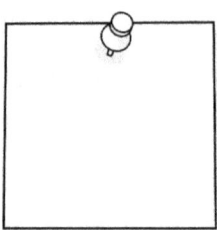

2.

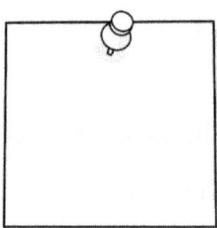

3.

EARLY LIFE LEADERSHIP NOTES

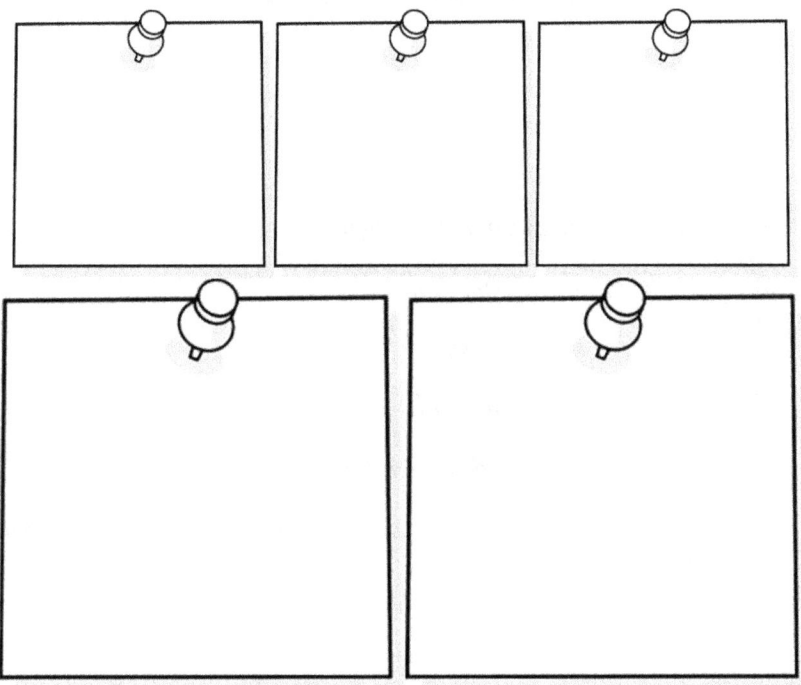

5: Research Procedure

1) Describe the research methodology,
2) provide sample information,
3) describe the instruments,
4) define independent variables and the dependent variables,
5) describe the research design and procedures, and
6) account for any ethical concerns pertaining to the research proposed.

Statically, a regression analysis was employed in order to determine if personality traits are a predictor of leadership skills in small children when controlling for previous formal schooling, gender, and language. I used IBM's SPSS statistical software in this study.

Where did you find the children for this study?

The sample from this study came from students and teachers at La Joya Independent School District and Weslaco Independent School District. These school districts are located at the southernmost point of Texas. The majority of these children are Hispanic and came from low socioeconomic families. La Joya ISD has twenty-three elementary schools, of which sixteen participated. Weslaco ISD has eleven elementary schools, and all eleven schools participated.

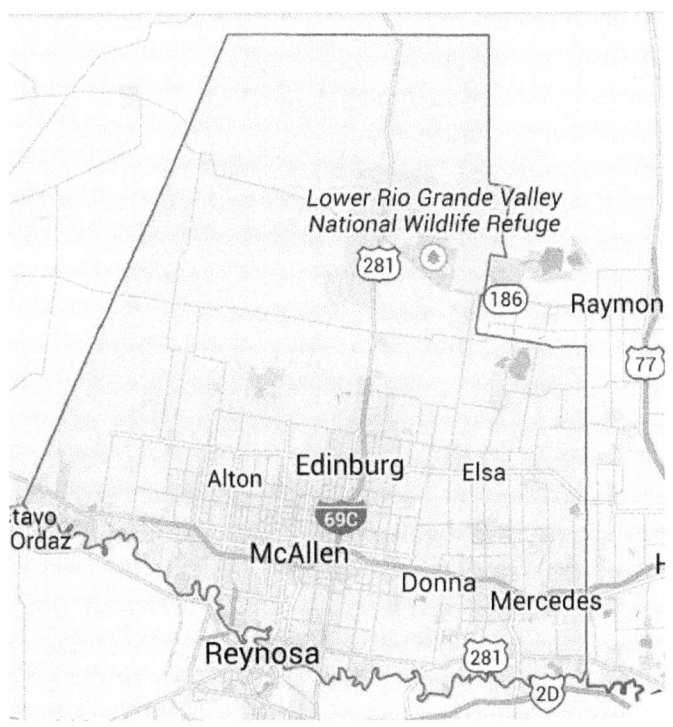

Hidalgo County
(https://www.tceq.texas.gov)

Above is a map of Texas. The bold outlined portion highlights Hidalgo County where the study took place, and the stars denote the La Joya (Left) and Weslaco Independent School Districts (Right). Because both school districts border Mexico, the population is predominantly Hispanic.

Hidalgo County
(https://en.wikipedia.org/wiki/Hidalgo_County,_Texas)

Methodology

All campuses involved in the study had one English-based kindergarten teacher participate from each of their participating campuses. Weslaco ISD had a total of 211 sets of surveys returned (N=211). La Joya ISD had sixteen English-based kindergarten teachers volunteer out of their twenty-three elementary schools (N=274). Together, there were 485 (N=485) sets of surveys completed.

In this study, 485 surveys were completed based on the kindergarten teachers' perceptions of their students. All school districts in Cameron and Hidalgo County were solicited, and letters of participation from the superintendents were collected. Once a school district agreed to participate, principals were also solicited to participate by recommending a kindergarten teacher. Although principals recommended a teacher to participate in this study, the teacher's participation was strictly voluntary. The teacher completed one set of surveys for each student on their classroom roster, and completed surveys and consent forms were collected and returned to me.

An individual regression analysis was conducted on each research question using the *Stepwise Method*. The graph that follows illustrates district participation: the first bar shows Weslaco Independent School District, with 211 student surveys completed; and the second shows La Joya Independent School District, with 274 student surveys completed.

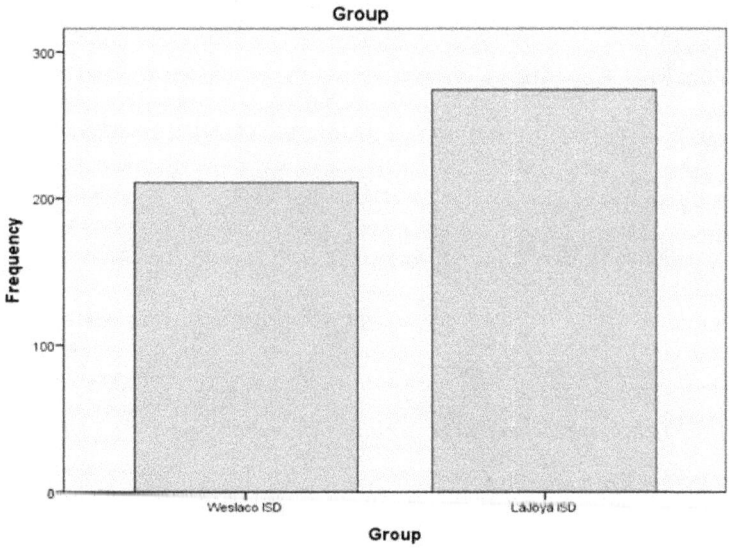

Survey Information in Depth

Surveys utilized the nine-question composite *Leadership Skills Checklist* (Castillo, 2001) and the 42 question *Big Five Inventory*, which identifies personality traits. In addition, teachers were asked the following:

1. *If the student received previous formal schooling*
2. *Details of the student's gender*
3. *If the student was bilingual*

Dependent Variable: Leadership Skills Checklist (Castillo, 2001)

The checklist was intended for the classroom teacher to use in order to help them discover their students' leadership abilities within nine areas:

1. *Possesses good communication skills, which include articulating clearly so that others understand and respond*
2. *Is willing to take on extra responsibility and extracurricular activities, such as sports*
3. *Encourages others' ideas and is willing to change own ideas if better ones are presented*
4. *Is looked up to by other students as a "leader" in activities such as sports or cooperative learning*
5. *Delegates—such as in a class project or setting roles in a game*

6. *Has confidence—can argue a point or issue, is an overachiever, seems to handle peer pressure well, and is self-motivated to learn or complete tasks*
7. *Is flexible and can adapt to new and different situations*
8. *Takes risks and is not afraid to express a thought in front of others or to experience change*
9. *Is dependable—can be trusted because they are consistent in following through*

(Castillo, 2001)

After completing the *Leadership Skills Checklist*, educators can determine strengths and weaknesses in the leadership of the child (Castillo, 2001).

Independent Variable: Big Five Personality Traits

Based in the University of California at Berkeley Personality Lab, Oliver P. John holds the rights to *The Big Five Personality Traits Inventory*. Allport and Odbert in 1936 and Norman in 1967 classified the terms of personality into categories, which were then clearly defined by John, Chaplin, and Goldberg to form what quickly became known as The Big Five Personality Traits. Goldberg (1981) conducted study after study to validate results, going from 1,710 traits to four hundred and seventy-five, then to fifty (John, Naumann & Soto, 2008).

The Big Five Personality Inventory is now a forty-four item self-report inventory designed to assess The Big Five Personality Traits which, as we have seen in previous chapters, are extraversion, agreeableness, conscientiousness, neuroticism, and openness. Extraversion was the most consistently related to leadership in adults (Judge, Bono, Ilies & Gerhardt, 2002). I wondered if this would be the case for children, as neuroticism and low extraversion were connected to social shyness in adults and relationships like these were also consistently found throughout childhood (Asendorpf & Van Aken, 2002).

Researchers link *The Big Five Personality Traits* with behavior problems identified in childhood. In one study, eighty-six children ranged in ages from nine to thirteen were studied. The results indicate the following:

1. Children with low scores in agreeableness and conscientiousness exhibit social problems, conduct problems, have attention deficits and display hyperactivity.

2. Children with low scores in openness to experience suffer problems with social behavior, conduct, and attention.

3. Neuroticism is associated with anxiety and depression.

(Ehrler, Evans & McGee, 1999).

Control Variables in Depth

As previously discussed, the variables that were controlled in this study are previous formal schooling, gender, and language, due to their potential to affect the results of the study. However, age, grade level, socioeconomic level, and ethnicity were not controlled. Since this study takes place in the Rio Grande Valley, ethnicity and socioeconomic level were not controlled due to insufficient variance. Most schools within the area are located in predominately socioeconomically low Hispanic communities. Please see the chart below for a breakdown of other variables and whether they were considered.

Rationale: Control Variable			
Variable	Range of Variability	Justification	Current Control Variable?
Student's Age	Limited Variability	All the students were in the same age group.	No
Student's Grade Level	Limited Variability	All the students were in the same grade.	No
Student's Ethnicity	Limited Variability	All students were predominantly the same race.	No
Poverty / Student's Socioeconomic Level	Limited Variability	According to the Census and Texas Education Agency, most students in this area are of low socioeconomic status.	No
Student's Gender	Variability	Hypothesis 1: There will be a difference between boys and girls with regard to leadership traits. Research: There is no significant research that states there is a difference between boys and girls with regard to leadership traits. A large study in New Zealand confirmed gender differences in leadership styles, defining the girls' leadership styles as directorial and the boys' leadership styles as dictatorial (Mawson, 2011).	Yes
Student's Language: Is the student Bilingual?	Variability	This study requested to work with one English kindergarten class from every campus within participating school districts, and because research on Hispanic leadership in children is severely limited, I also wanted to be culturally sensitive to the Hispanic population (Irby & Lara-Alecio, 1996).	Yes
Student's Previous Schooling	Variability	Hypothesis 2: There will be a difference between students who have had previous formal schooling or pre-kinder. Research: Research shows that pre-kindergarten classrooms increase pre-academic and social skills (Burchinal, Howes, Pianta, Bryant, Early, Clifford, & Barbarin, 2008). Ultimately, certain findings stated that the quality of instruction makes a child successful in kindergarten, not previous formal schooling (Burchinal et al., 2008). Additionally, some research found both at-risk and not at-risk students to be performing at similar levels in pre-academic skills (Lamon, 2005). Although short-term research presents positive results in support of full-day kindergarten sessions, the results were limited and mixed with regard to long-term impacts (Schoenfeldt, 2012). There is a bounty of argumentative data; therefore, we will control for previous formal schooling.	Yes

Research Design & Procedures

The purpose of this study was to prove that children possess leadership skills and capabilities. Participating teachers received an envelope with sets of surveys and filled out one set for each student based on their perception of that child. The surveys were then collected and entered into an Excel program spreadsheet, which was uploaded to SPSS. I ran the descriptive statistics, a *Pearson Correlation*, and t-test, then a multiple regression, using the Stepwise method, which was used because it is an automated tool used to identify a useful subset of predictors. This process systematically adds the most significant variable or removes the least significant variable during each step (http://people.duke.edu/~rnau/regstep.htm, 2016).

A statistical analysis was completed to determine if there was a relationship between the child's personality traits and leadership skills when controlling for previous formal schooling, gender, and language. This study was based solely on the teacher's perception of the student, and students were in no way involved, questioned, or identified. Teachers received directions. School districts from Port Isabel to Rio Grande City were solicited to participate in this study, but La Joya Independent School District and Weslaco Independent School District agreed to participate. Then an email was set out to all elementary school principals within those school districts. Participating teachers were recommended by principals who chose to participate in this research. Teachers received an envelope from their principal with twenty-five sets of surveys and completed one set for each student on their kindergarten rosters. Directions and a short welcome letter were included (see appendix). Surveys were collected by the district administration and returned to the researcher.

For hypotheses and hypothesis testing, data was computed through SPSS to decipher the relationships among variables. The null hypothesis was rejected for all nine research questions. They were all significant. A multiple regression analysis was used to determine if a relationship exists between the dependent variables—openness, consciousness, extroversion, agreeableness, and neuroticism (otherwise known as *The Big Five Personality Traits*)—and the independent variables (otherwise known as the *Leadership Skills Checklist*) of communication, responsibility, the ability to encourage others, being viewed as a leader by others, the ability to delegate duties and responsibilities to cultivate a teamwork approach, confidence, flexibility, the ability to adapt to new and different situations, risk-taking, not being afraid of change, and dependability.

Ethical Considerations

There were six ethical considerations made in this study:

1. Campus principals selected the participating teachers.
2. All teacher participation was voluntary.
3. No incentives were offered for participating.

4. Participants could withdraw from the study at any time without penalty.

5. Kindergarten parents were not notified, because teachers completed surveys.

6. This study was IRB-approved. The school district and teacher participation were strictly voluntary, and all teachers signed a consent form.

EARLY LIFE LEADERSHIP NOTES

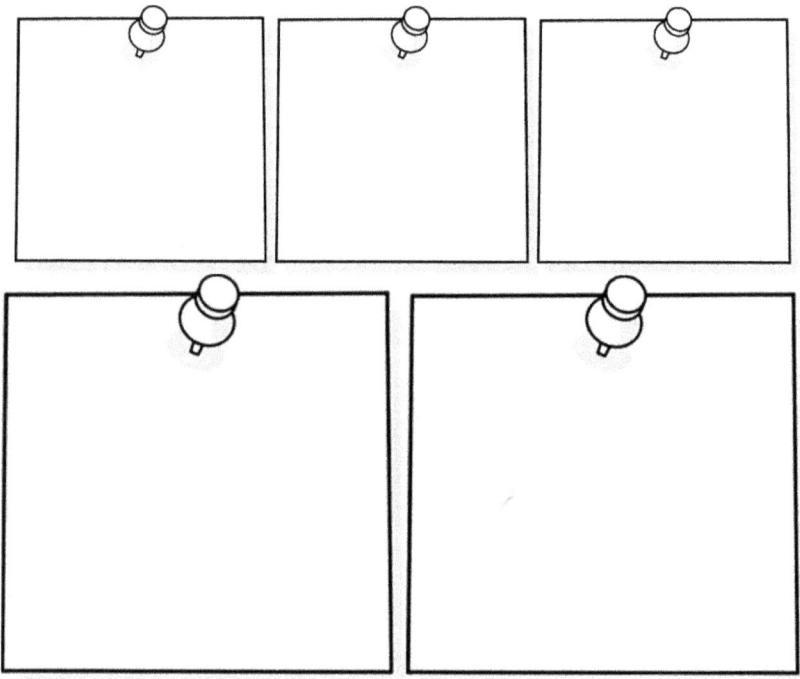

6: Results

The purpose of this chapter is to report the data collection process, descriptive statistics, and null hypotheses tested, provide the description of the data process, and illustrate the results of the data analysis. In this study, I was trying to determine if a predictable relationship exists between leadership skills and personality traits in kindergarteners. Each of the nine leadership skills on the *Leadership Skills Checklist* was defined as a research question, including the *Leadership Skills Checklist*'s total composite scores.

Figure 2 illustrates the distribution of completed survey sets per participating campus:

Figure 2. Distribution of campus surveys completed

In this study, 485 surveys were completed, and any missing information was coded 999. As previously stated, common control variables such as age and grade level were not surveyed due to limited variability. The first demographic question on the survey was the control variable of previous formal schooling. Even though 485 survey sets were completed, not all teachers answered this question, and from this, one can infer that teachers were uncertain of some students' past educational experiences. These blank questions were coded 999.

Figure 3 illustrates that 86.7% of kindergarteners had received pre-kindergarten education or formal education from a private preschool:

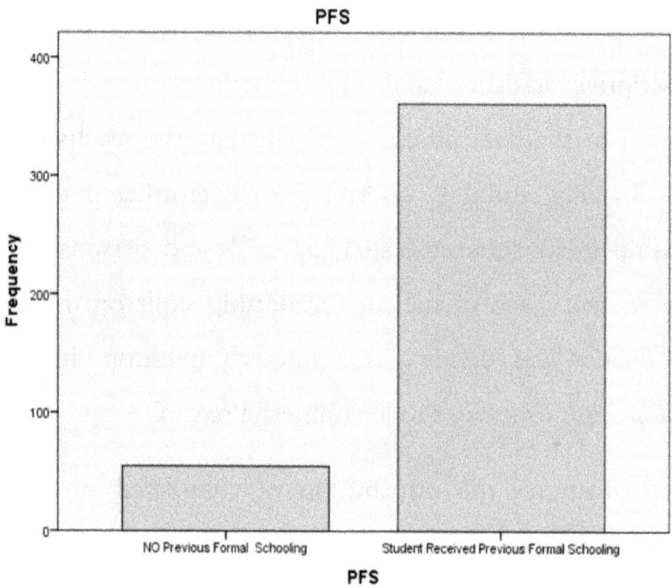

Figure 3: Distribution of students who had previous formal schooling

The second demographic surveyed was gender. In chapter 2, we saw that existing research on children and gender was inconclusive. Thus, the study controlled for gender. Figure 4 illustrates the distribution of students' gender. There were 197 females and 233 males in this study.

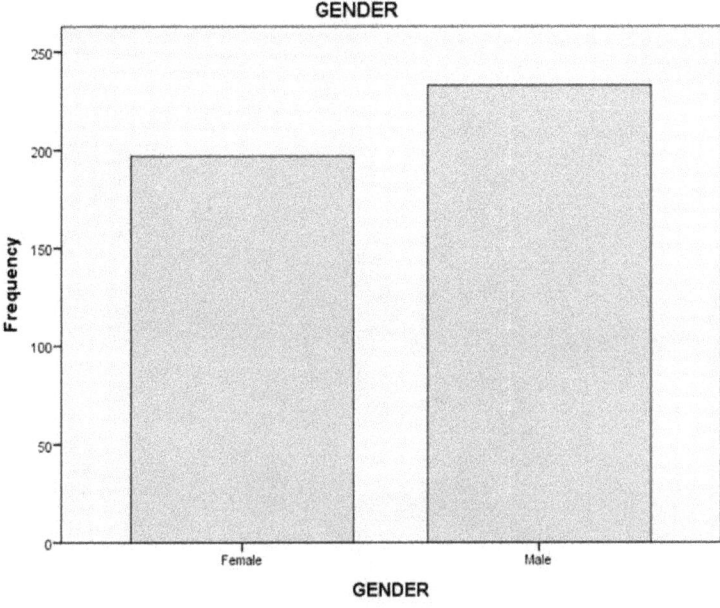

Figure 4: Distribution of gender

The third demographic surveyed was the control variable of language. As discussed, language was a control variable because the student population in this area is predominantly Hispanic, and both school districts border Mexico. Although all teachers that participated were assigned to English-speaking kindergarten classrooms, the cultural ties to Spanish in some students were so strong that language might otherwise have had a significant impact on the outcomes of this study. Figure 5 illustrates that 25.53% were noted bilingual by their teacher, and 74.46% were not:

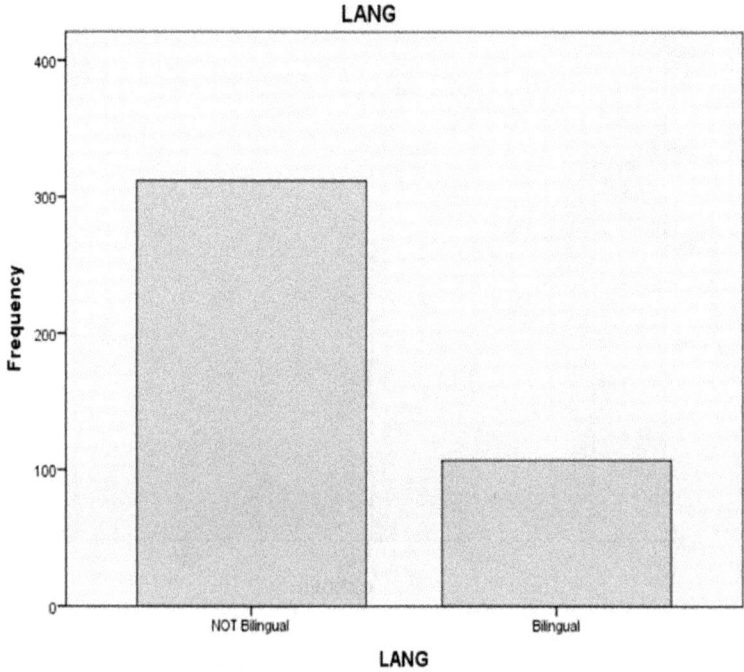

Figure 5: Distribution of students who were bilingual

Teachers check off if their students were bilingual or not. Although it was very clear that English based classrooms were requested to participate in this study, some classroom students were noted to be bilingual.

The graph titled CKL Composite (Leadership Skills Check List) shows the distribution of composite scores for the *Leadership Skills Checklist*. The average score on a scale from 1-4 was 2.73. The score that was repeated the most reported score was 4.00, as shown in the graph.

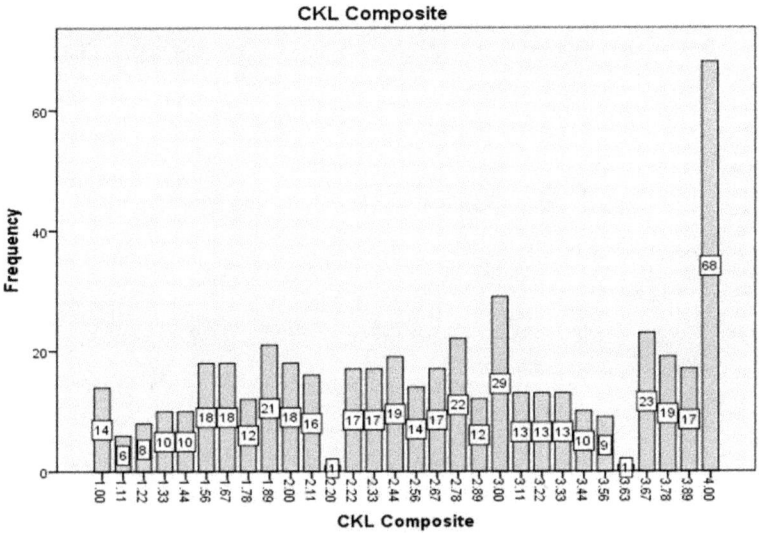

Figure 11: Distribution of composite scores for the Leadership Skills Checklist

	CK1 COMM	CK2 RESP	CK3 ENCOUR	CK4 LK UP LED	CK5 DELEG	CK6 CONF	CK7 FLEX	CK8 RK TAKE	CK9 DEP	COM 1-9	OPEN	CON	EXT	AGR	NEU
CK1 COMM	1														
CK2 RESP	.604**	1													
CK3 ENCOUR	.668**	.768**	1												
CK4 LK UP LED	.713**	.759**	.813*	1											
CK5 DELEG	.683**	.708**	.774*	.832**	1										
CK6 CONF	.708**	.630**	.702*	.730**	.717**	1									
CK7 FLEX	.658**	.617**	.717*	.685**	.677**	.707**	1								
CK8 RISK TK	.634**	.647**	.682*	.702**	.677**	.723**	.638**	1							
CK9 DEP	.615**	.676**	.726*	.712**	.706**	.617**	.751**	.561**	1						
COMP 1-9	.837**	.850**	.901*	.907**	.884**	.846**	.832**	.814**	.826**	1					
OPEN	.658**	.604**	.668*	.832**	.623**	.684**	.628**	.639**	.604**	.753**	1				
CON	.544**	.603**	.634*	.632**	.625**	.521**	.618**	.414**	.746**	.694**	.629**	1			
EXT	.466**	.419**	.411*	.435**	.406**	.562**	.343**	.593**	.231**	.501**	.531**	.157**	1		
AGR	.287**	.349**	.406*	.435**	.354**	.262**	.479**	.174**	.538**	.412**	.306**	.624**	-.077	1	
NEU	-.300**	-.354**	-.365*	-.364**	-.355**	-.400**	-.483**	-.326**	-.403**	-.433**	-.343**	-.479**	-.251**	-.582**	1

Don't be scared by this graph. It is okay if you don't understand it, and can be quite difficult to do so, but I have placed it here because it shows all those statistics we talked about above at a glance. It is called a *Pearson Correlation*. Results revealed that a significant relationship existed between all research questions (1-10) and all personality traits. The higher the number you see, the stronger the relationship that exists between the top and the side variables (x and the y-axis).

Results of Statistical Analysis

This section explains the results of the regression analysis conducted to determine if a predictable relationship exists between the dependent variables (*The Big Five Personality Traits*) and independent variables (*Leadership Skills Checklist*). Categorical variables that included two categories (e.g., gender) were dummy-coded a zero (female) or a one (male) to examine through a t-test to find the difference between means. Correlation analysis was run on continuous variables (e.g., *Leadership Skills Checklist* scores) to determine the strength and direction of each relationship. Only significant data was reported.

The first research question—"Is there a relationship between personality traits and communication_in kindergarten students when controlling for (1) student gender, (2) previous education, and (3) language?"—is a combination of all nine research questions together as one variable. A regression analysis was conducted in SPSS in order to determine the strength of the relationship that exists between personality traits and all nine leadership skills. The graph below illustrates the composite scores. The mean was 2.73 (1-4).

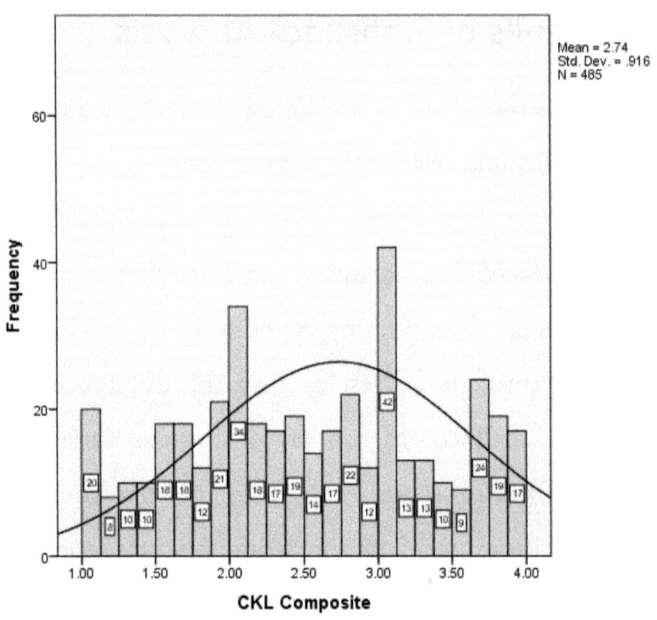

DID PREVIOUS FORMAL SCHOOLING HAVE AN EFFECT ON CHILDREN'S LEADERSHIP SKILLS?

The t-test revealed that students who received previous formal schooling were rated higher on the *Leadership Skills Checklist* than those who did not.

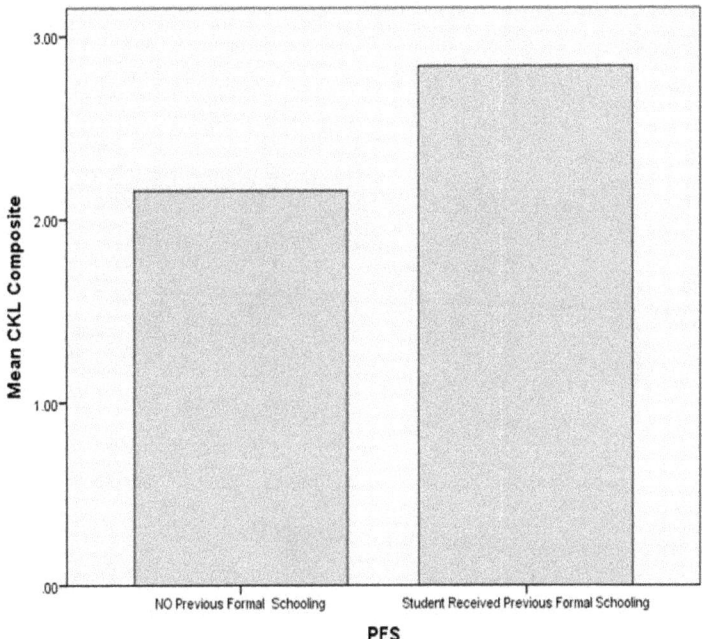

DID GENDER HAVE AN EFFECT ON CHILDREN'S LEADERSHIP SKILLS?

The t-test revealed that female students were rated higher on the *Leadership Skills Checklist* than males.

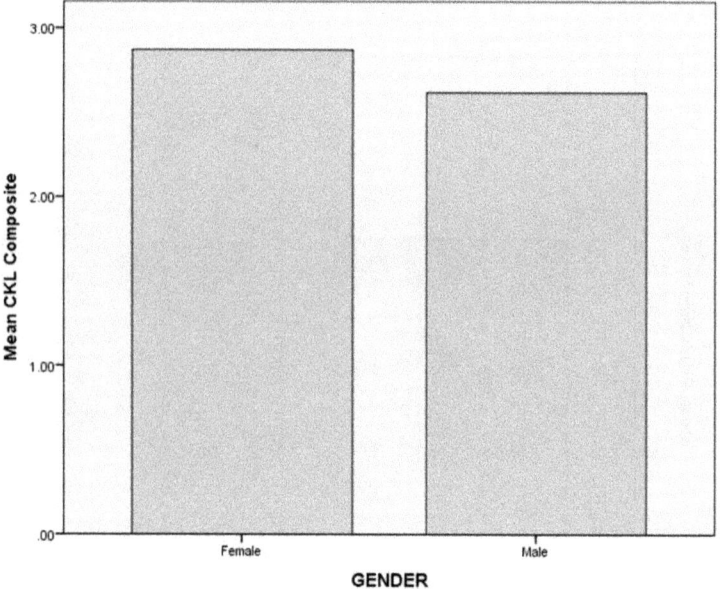

DID LANGUAGE HAVE AN EFFECT ON CHILDREN'S LEADERSHIP SKILLS?

The t-test revealed that students who were not bilingual were rated higher on the *Leadership Skills Checklist* than students who were bilingual.

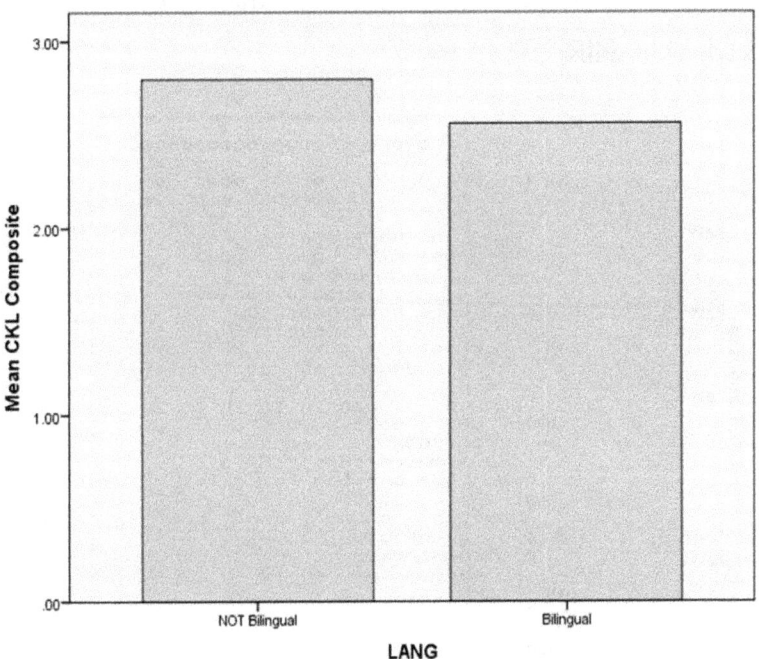

RELATIONSHIP BETWEEN SURVEYS AND PERSONALITY VARIABLES

The graph below illustrates the relationship between the composite questions and the personality variable of openness. The higher students were rated on the *Leadership Skills Checklist*, the higher they were rated in terms of openness by their teachers, and the higher they were rated on leadership skills.

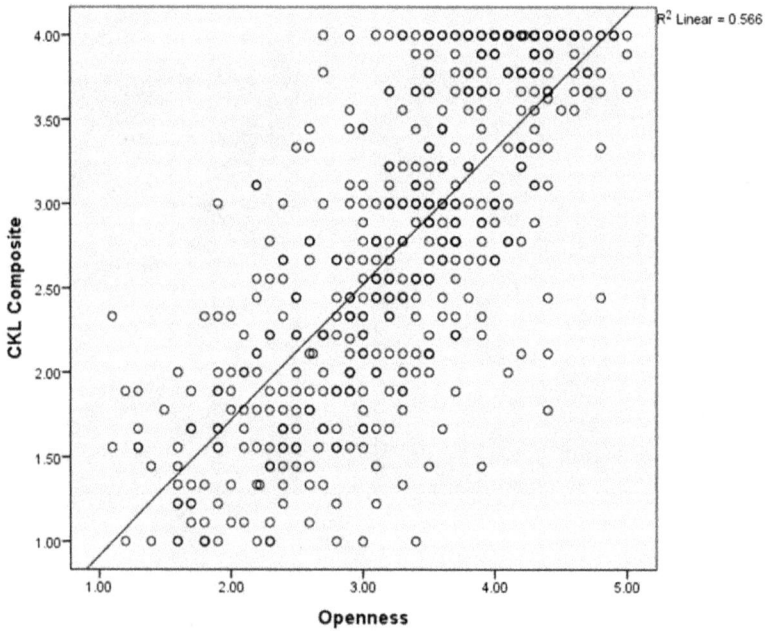

The graph below illustrates the relationship between the composite questions and the personality variable of conscientiousness. The higher students were rated on the *Leadership Skills Checklist*, the higher they were rated in terms of conscientiousness by their teachers.

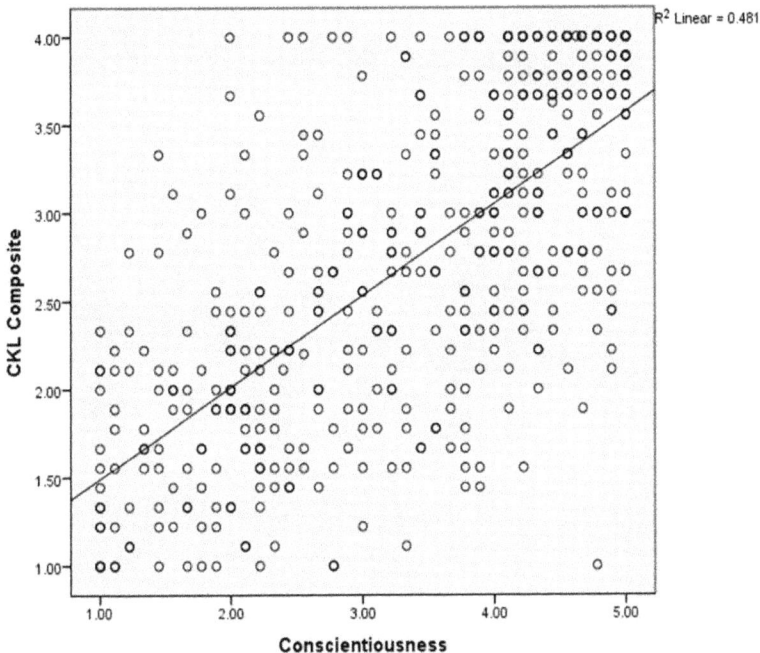

The graph below illustrates the relationship between the composite questions and the personality variable of extraversion. The higher students were rated on the *Leadership Skills Checklist*, the higher they were rated in terms of extraversion by their teachers.

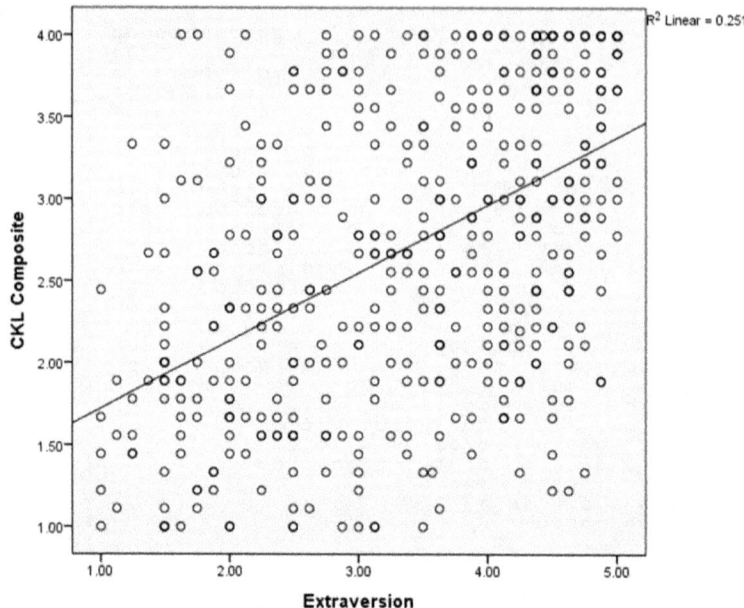

The graph below illustrates the relationship between the composite questions and the personality variable of agreeableness. The higher students were rated on the *Leadership Skills Checklist*, the higher they were rated in terms of agreeableness by their teachers.

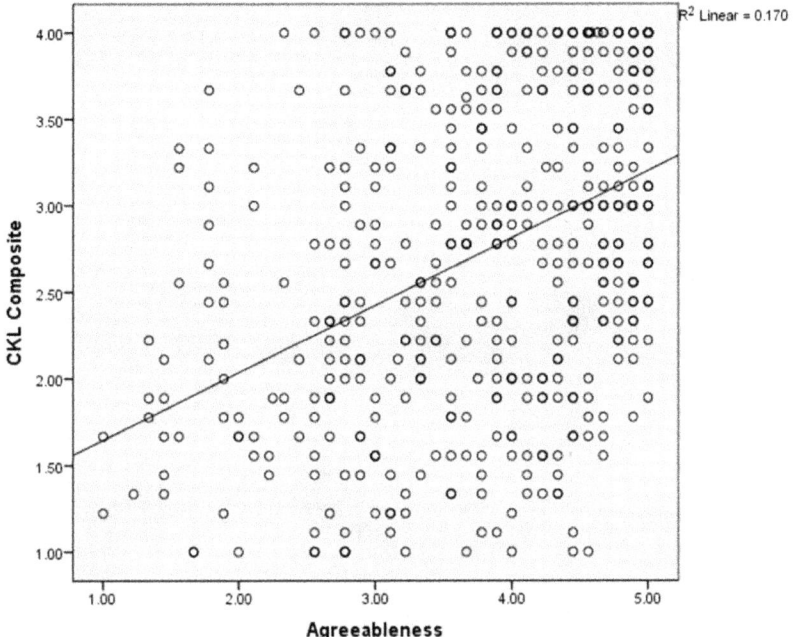

This model shows the relationship between communication, *The Big Five Personality Traits,* and the control variables. Based on the results, the analysis revealed that students who received previous formal schooling were rated higher on communication by their teachers than students who did not.

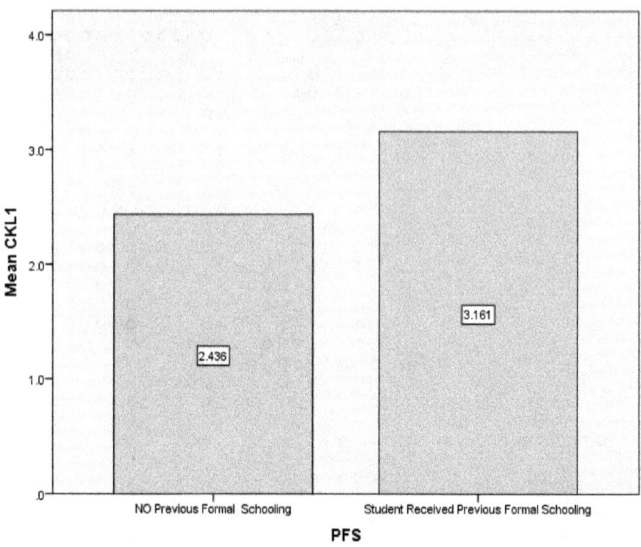

This analysis revealed that students who were not bilingual were rated higher by teachers on communication than students who were bilingual.

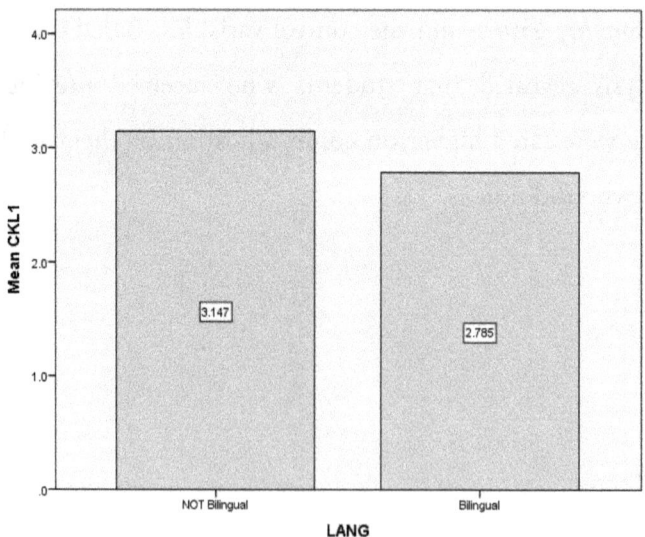

The third predictor was gender. The analysis revealed that teachers rated female students higher than males in terms of communication. The first three variables were all control variables and were all significant.

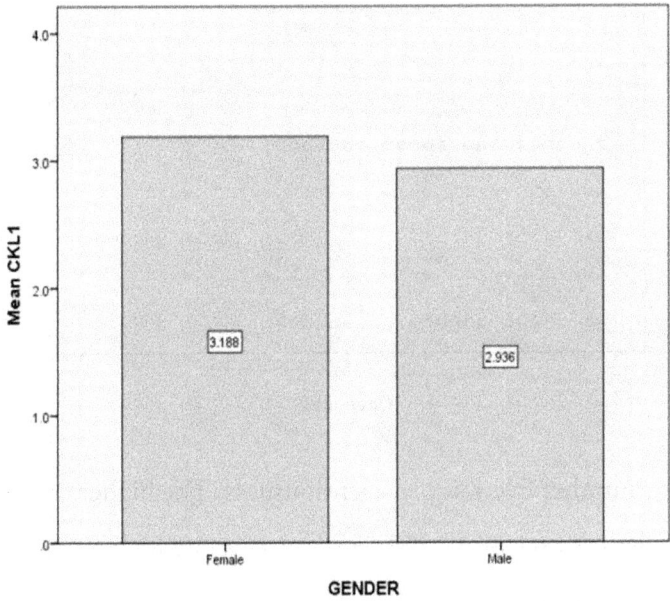

The data showed that the higher teachers rated students in terms of openness, the higher their rating was in terms of communication.

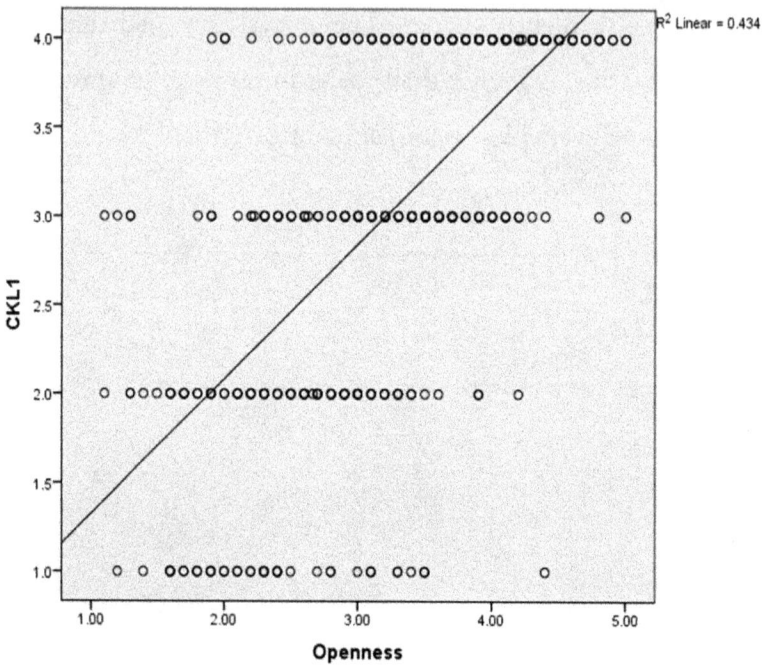

Predictor number five was conscientiousness. The higher teachers rated their students in terms of conscientiousness, the higher the rating was in terms of communication.

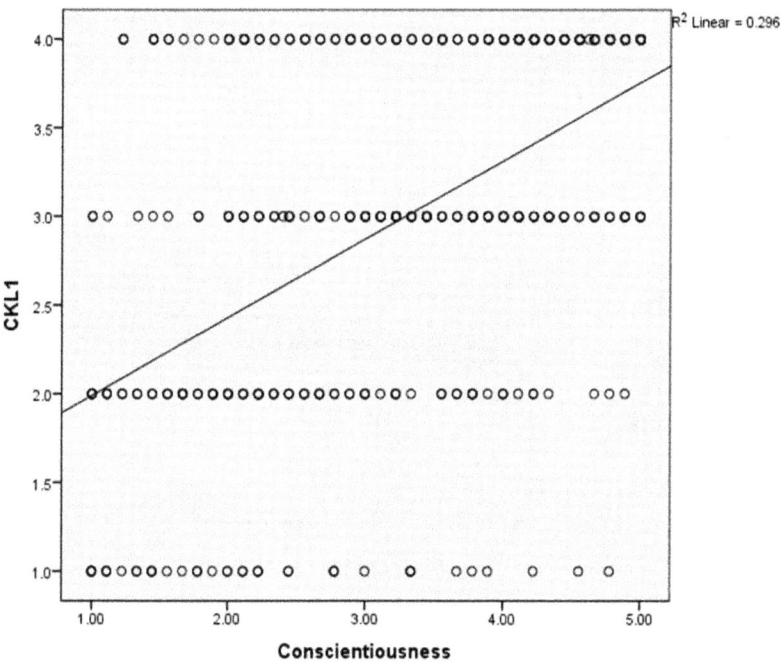

Predictor six was extraversion. The higher teachers rated their students in terms of extraversion, the higher their rating was in terms of communication

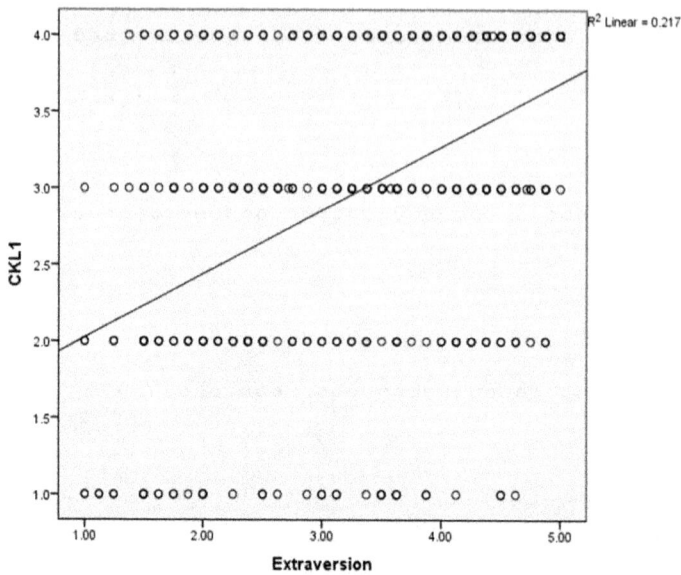

The analysis revealed that students who received previous formal schooling were rated higher in responsibility than their peers.

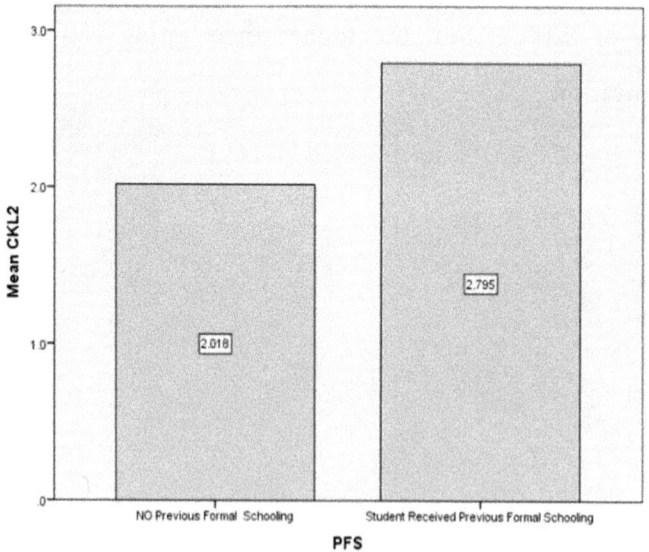

EARLY LIFE LEADERSHIP NOTES

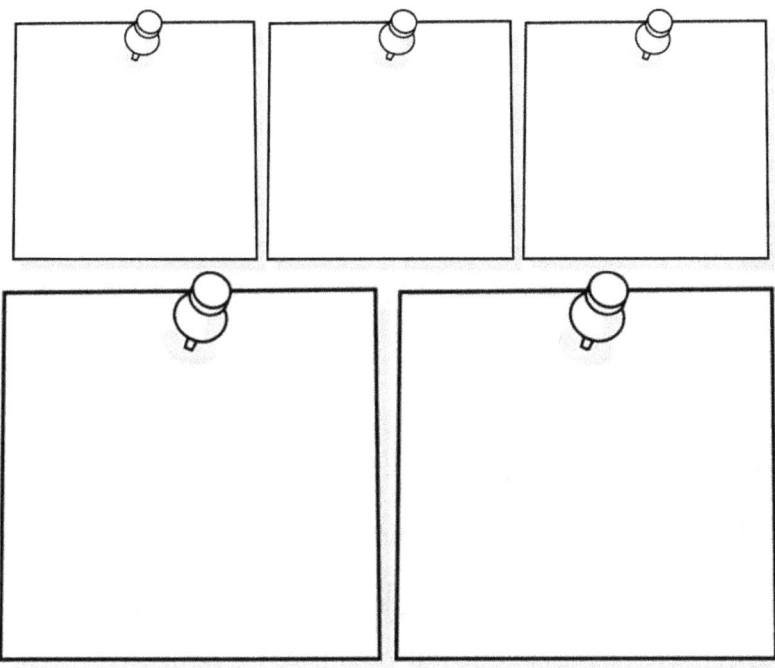

7: Research Findings

The purpose of this study was to dig deeper and attempt to find an answer to the question, "Where do leaders come from?"

I attempted to do so by examining the relationship between personality traits and leadership skills in kindergarten students. *The Big Five Inventory* was used to measure personality traits, and the *Leadership Skill Checklist* was used to measure leadership skills.

The second purpose of this study was to test the assumption that children *do* possess leadership skills and have the capacity to be leaders. Here, we will discuss the findings, implications, recommended research, limitations, and final thoughts.

DISCUSSION OF FINDINGS

After completing the statistical analysis, it was found that the personality traits of neuroticism, language and agreeableness were the weakest predictors among these surveys and were the concepts that teachers saw less in their students. Openness, conscientiousness, and extraversion proved to be the most popular predictors of leadership skills, as well as the traits teachers saw most in their students. In addition, previous formal schooling and gender (in females) proved the strongest and most popular survey choices for teachers as they surveyed leadership in their students. Females were rated higher by their teachers in all nine leadership skills.

Survey Variables	Findings at a Glance
Previous Formal Schooling	Previous formal schooling emerged as a significant predictor of leadership skills. (In all 9 of the Leadership Skills Checklist questions)
Gender	Gender emerged as a significant predictor of leadership skills. (In all 9 of the *Leadership Skills Checklist* questions)
Language	Language emerged as a significant predictor of leadership skills. (In 4 out of 9 of the *Leadership Skills Checklist* questions)
Openness Conscientiousness	Openness and conscientiousness emerged as significant predictors of leadership skills. (In all 9 of the Leadership Skills Checklist questions)
Extraversion	Extraversion emerged as a significant predictor of leadership skills. (In 8 out of 9 of the *Leadership Skills Checklist* questions)

SUMMARY OF FINDINGS

I want to remind the reader that this study was conducted in South Texas among predominantly Hispanic children with a low socioeconomic level. If this study was repeated, you might get different responses based on household income, gender, race, and life and educational experiences. Although children don't see the color skin in a racial discrimination sense, they *learn* "color" and discrimination from the people around them, the images they see on TV, and other media sources.

As we saw in the previous chapters, adults who are perceived as extraverts are often also seen as better leaders, but that was not true for the children in this study. Teachers who perceived their students as being open and having high levels of conscientiousness rated them higher on the *Leadership Skills Checklist*. Students who are open to learning and trying new things may be perceived as stronger leaders, and those rated higher in conscientiousness may score higher on the *Checklist* because they may be more conscious of their behavior and learning.

In terms of gender, in the study, as in the previous chapters, more girls emerged as leaders in the classroom. This may be because girls are often seen as more eager to learn and tend to have fewer behavior problems than more stereotypically rambunctious boys.

If you look at the following graph, you will see the nine leadership skills at the top, the 10th column being the composite. The composite is the total number of points collected throughout questions 1-9. On the side column, the first three demographic questions are at the top, and below those are *The Big Five Personality Traits* we measured. Each filled box shows a relationship between the personality trait and leadership skill. If there is a blank, that means there was no significant relationship between that skill and that specific personality trait.

	COMM	RESP	ENC	LPF	DELG	CONF	FLX	RISK	DEP	COMP Q1-9
Leadership Skills Checklist Variables 1-9 — COMP Q1-9: The Total Composite Score of 1-9 Together										
PFS	$R^2=.060$	$R^2=.058$	$R^2=.033$	$R^2=.049$	$R^2=.066$	$R^2=.057$	$R^2=.034$	$R^2=.052$	$R^2=.025$	$R^2=.059$
GEN	$\Delta R^2=.021$	$\Delta R^2=.013$	$\Delta R^2=.015$	$\Delta R^2=.014$	$\Delta R^2=.035$	$\Delta R^2=.020$	$\Delta R^2=.018$	$\Delta R^2=.012$	$\Delta R^2=.013$	$\Delta R^2=.024$
LANG	$\Delta R^2=.027$					$\Delta R^2=.018$	$\Delta R^2=.017$			$\Delta R^2=.012$
OPEN	$\Delta R^2=.328$	$\Delta R^2=.011$	$\Delta R^2=.396$	$\Delta R^2=.414$	$\Delta R^2=.018$	$\Delta R^2=.363$	$\Delta R^2=.065$	$\Delta R^2=.350$	$\Delta R^2=.023$	$\Delta R^2=.469$
CONS	$\Delta R^2=.037$	$\Delta R^2=.353$	$\Delta R^2=.073$	$\Delta R^2=.060$	$\Delta R^2=.338$	$\Delta R^2=.035$	$\Delta R^2=.323$	$\Delta R^2=.009$	$\Delta R^2=.527$	$\Delta R^2=.085$
EXT	$\Delta R^2=.036$	$\Delta R^2=.082$	$\Delta R^2=.021$	$\Delta R^2=.017$	$\Delta R^2=.077$	$\Delta R^2=.052$	$\Delta R^2=.005$	$\Delta R^2=.084$		$\Delta R^2=.040$
AGRE			$\Delta R^2=.009$				$\Delta R^2=.011$		$\Delta R^2=.015$	$\Delta R^2=.006$
NEUR						$\Delta R^2=.011$	$\Delta R^2=.038$			

Figure 1. Variance Table

WHAT DOES THIS RESEARCH IMPLY?

This study was able to predict and respectfully document leadership skills in kindergarten students who possessed certain personality traits and revealed there is a relationship between personality traits and leadership skills in kindergarten students. Below is a breakdown of the conclusions found in all the research discussed over the course of this book.

Previous Formal Schooling

<u>The literature says</u>: Programs such as private pre-schools and pre-kindergartens were found to be important programs for all children, regardless of a child's background. These programs offered communication and socialization (Shipley, 1998).

<u>Research findings</u>: Similar to some literature reviewed, it was found that previous formal schooling was associated with leadership in some kindergarten children.

This research suggests we need to encourage children to attend private pre-schools or pre-kindergarten to help nurture leadership development in children.

Gender

The literature says: Girls were seen as emerging leaders and exhibited more leadership behaviors by asking more questions and leading more social interaction versus boys (Dhuey & Lipscomb, 2006; Yamaguchi, 2001).

Research findings: Parallel to the literature, **girls** were rated higher in terms of leadership by their teachers for all nine facets of leadership skills.

This indicates that some males may benefit from more leadership development activities.

Language

The literature says: Castillo found that dual language participants scored the same as non-dual language participants on the Leadership Skills Checklist (Castillo, 2001).

Research findings: Contrary to the literature, in this study, kindergarteners who were not bilingual were rated higher in terms of leadership skills by their teachers than students who were bilingual.

This implies that some bilingual students could benefit from leadership development activities and may be seen as struggling learners.

Openness

The literature says: Openness has been shown to be linked to knowledge and achievement and is modestly correlated with cognitive ability (Educational Testing Service, 2012).

Research findings: Teachers recognized leadership skills in kindergarten students who were rated higher in terms of openness.

Teachers may have rated students higher in terms of leadership if they demonstrated good academic grades and were open to learning and new activities.

Conscientiousness

The literature says: Conscientiousness has been shown to have a positive correlation with achievement-striving, self-discipline, diligence, achievement via independence, and maybe a particularly strong predictor of academic achievement (Educational Testing Service, 2012). Children who are conscientious seek and provide advice, and exhibit social skills, intelligence, and ambition (Markey, Markey & Tinsley, 2004).

Research findings: Teachers recognized leadership skills in kindergarten students who were rated higher in terms of conscientiousness.

Teachers might have rated students higher in leadership if they demonstrated social skills, self-discipline, self-monitoring, and intelligence.

Extraversion

The literature says: Extraversion in youth has been shown to have a positive correlation with academic success, and the number of clubs and organizations the participant belonged to were a significant factor in determining leadership (Educational Testing Service, 2012; Parmer, 2012). In childhood, extraversion might include outspokenness and being socially confident, verbally fluent, and assertive (Hampson & Goldberg, 2006).

Research findings: Teachers recognized leadership skills in kindergarten students who were rated higher in terms of extraversion.

Teachers might have rated students higher in terms of leadership if they demonstrated confidence, sociability, and strong verbal skills.

Implications for the Classroom Teacher

Based on the results of this study, teachers may need professional development in the areas of:

1. identifying leadership skills vs. personality traits;
2. realizing the benefits of previous formal schooling;
3. implementing leadership strategies for bilingual students;
4. acknowledging and addressing gender differences in the classroom;

5. understanding how to teach leadership skills in the classroom.

More to Think About

✓ Previous formal schooling may potentially increase leadership skills in some kindergarten children.

✓ Gender results of this study suggest some males may benefit from leadership skill development.

✓ Language results of this study suggest bilingual students need leadership skill development.

✓ Openness & Conscientiousness: Teachers recognized leadership skills (communication skills, responsibility, the ability to encourage others, being viewed as a leader by others, delegation, confidence, flexibility, risk-taking, and dependability) in kindergarten students who were rated higher in openness and conscientiousness.

✓ Extraversion: Teachers recognized leadership skills in kindergarten students who were rated higher on extraversion.

✓ Based on the results of this study, teachers (1) may have rated students higher in terms of leadership skills if they demonstrated good behavior and academic grades, and (2) may need professional development.

Research Limitations

There were six limitations to this study:

1. I am employed by one of the participating school districts.

2. I worked for one of the participating campuses during this study.

3. The surveys completed were based on the teacher's perception of the student alone.

4. I could not control for teacher biases.

Early Life Leadership Spotlight

There were three key objectives this study aimed to bring to light:

1. *To provide acknowledgment of the presence of leadership skills in children*

2. *To provide research to a limited body of knowledge*

3. *To bring awareness to child leadership in hopes of growing stronger and more ethical leaders*

EARLY LIFE LEADERSHIP NOTES

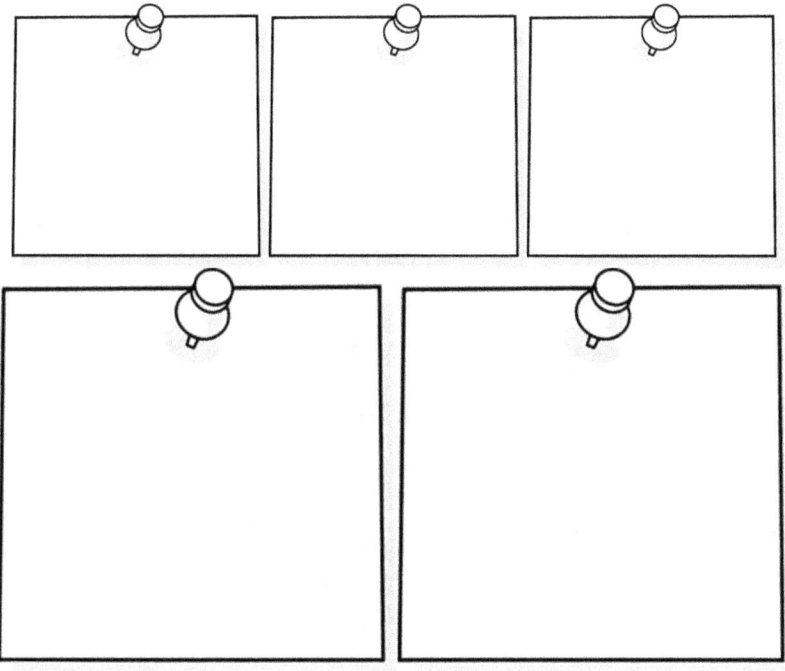

8: So, Where Do Leaders Come From?

This research proves the need to conduct more research in the area of children and leadership.

As for where leaders come from, leaders come from two places. The first place leaders come from is nature. Leaders are born with personality traits and DNA that dictates they become leaders. It comes naturally. Where others do not have the desire to be leaders, they feel more comfortable following. Some of us are born risk-takers while others are just more conservative. If you watch children play, born leaders will always rise to the top and take over. You may hear them say, "Hey, you do this, and you do that!" or "I'm the teacher, and you are the student!"

The second place leaders come from is development. Some leaders are developed through training, experience, mentorship, and education. Everyone has the opportunity to learn about leadership, whether that's from coaches, parents, pastors or teachers. Children learn leadership from the adults in their lives who are close to them, not pop stars or athletes! They look to you to learn leadership skills—though these may not always be obvious—so be intentional about the leadership lessons that you teach the children in your life and help them grow. There's nothing wrong with talking to them about attending a leadership camp or encouraging them to find a need in their community and take charge of it, even if it's as small as collecting socks for the local shelter.

Leaders are both born and developed. The argument among some scholars about the truth of that statement is never-ending, but that's what I believe according to my research and my experiences (however, I would love to hear your thoughts! Email christinademara@gmail.com).

In conclusion, we need to leave our stereotypes, low expectations, and the little red schoolhouse behind and move toward a new world of education that connects children to real-world constructs like leadership. This research was my humble attempt to provide parents, adults, and educators with the information they need to understand, identify and make knowledgeable decisions regarding leadership in children regardless of their gender, ethnicity, or social status (Pramling Samuelsson & Kaga, 2008).

EARLY LIFE LEADERSHIP NOTES

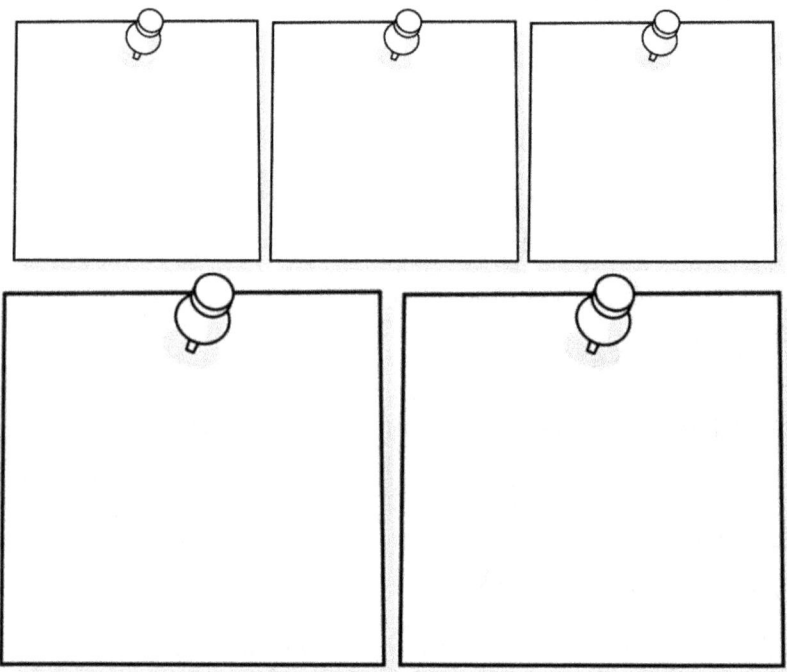

Bless This Book!

If you enjoyed this book or any other of Christina's books, your honest review is greatly appreciated! Reviews help the author's books be seen by others and help the writer qualify for different book promotions.

Your Time and Review is Appreciated!

Questions?

ChristinaDeMara.com
EarlyLifeLeadership.com
christinademara@gmail.com

BONUS #1!

Start here with a FREE eBook!
Early Life Leadership in the Classroom
is free on Amazon and Kobo.
This is a delightful starting point.

BONUS #2!

Free Copy of the
Meaningful Teacher Leadership Grid
***Available at **Barnes & Noble**
and **Amazon*****

Memorization Icon	"OW" Leadership Reflection	Internalization What does that look like? Draw a picture or symbol.	What do I need to do to nurture this area?
	Know: What do I know about Leadership?		
	Glow: How do I stand out?		
	Show: What do I show others? How do others perceive me?		
	Grow: How am I growing as a leader? What am I doing to better my leadership skills?		
	Snow: What is cold in my leadership life and requires attention?		
	Bow: What am I ready to launch forward?		
	Low: What is an area of weakness I need to work on?		
	Sow: What am I working on? Remember, you reap what you sow		
	Row: What am I rowing toward? Am I going in the right direction?		
	Owe: Whom do I owe for mentoring me? What am I taking away from my mentors?		
	Bowl: What is in my bowl? What leadership resources do I have available to me?		
	Mow: What is mowing me down and stopping me from moving to the next level of leadership greatness?		
	Flow: What is flowing smoothly? What are the things going well in the leadership aspect of my life?		
	Tow: What am I towing that may be slowing me down from reaching my full leadership potential?		

Please Connect with Christina!

She would love to hear from you!

Christina has two Facebook groups called
I Love Reading & Writing
and
I Love Leadership
for her readers.

You are welcome to join!

References

Ackerman, D., & Barnett, W. (2005). Prepared for Kindergarten: What Does "Readiness" Mean? Preschool Policy Brief for the National Institute for Early Education Research, 13-13.

Addison, L., Oliver, A. I., & Cooper, C. R. (1987). Developing leadership potential in gifted children and youth. Reston, VA: ERIC Clearinghouse on Handicapped and Gifted Children.

Andersen, L. (2011). The effects of formal leadership-lessons on the emergence of positive social-leadership skills of pre-kindergarten students.

Asendorpf, J. B., & Van Aken, M. A. G. (2002). Validity of big five personality judgments in childhood: A 9-year longitudinal study; 17: 1-17 (2003).

Ayman, R., & Korabik, K. (2010). Leadership: Why gender and culture matter. American Psychologist, 65(3), 157.

Berkowitz, M. (2009). Character education and gifted children. High Ability Studies, 20(2), 131-142.

Bisland, A. (January 1, 2004). Developing Leadership Skills in Young Gifted Students. The Gifted Child Today, 27, 24-31.

Bohlin, L. C. (2000). Determinants of young children's leadership and dominance strategies during play. (9993607, Indiana University). ProQuest Dissertations and Theses. 139-139 p. Retrieved from http://search.proquest.com/docview/304624371?accountid=7058. (304624371).

Boseovski, J. J., Shallwani, S., & Lee, K. (2009). It's all good: Children's personality attributions after repeated success and failure in peer and computer interactions. British Journal of Developmental Psychology, 27(4), 783-797.

Boulais, N. A., & University of Mississippi. (2001). A content analysis of children's literature using Kouzes and Posner's leadership themes in the Caldecott Medal winners and selected honor books.

Brenner, S. C. (1991). Leadership characteristics in young children as perceived by caregivers in a child care setting. Philadelphia, PA.

Burchinal, M., Howes, C., Pianta, R., Bryant, D., Early, D., Clifford, R., & Barbarin, O. (2008). Predicting child outcomes at the end of kindergarten from the quality of pre-kindergarten teacher-child interactions and instruction. Applied Developmental Science, 12(3), 140-153.

Campbell, R. (2007, January 1). Leadership: Getting It Done. Retrieved September 6, 2014, from http://web.missouri.edu/~campbellr/Leadership/chapter4.htm

Carver, C. L. (2012). Developing Leadership Content Knowledge during School Leader Preparation. International Journal of Educational Leadership Preparation, 7(3),

Caspi, A., Harrington, H., Milne, B., Amell, J. W., Theodore, R. F., & Moffitt, T. E. (2003). Children's behavioral styles at age 3 are linked to their adult personality traits at age 26. Journal of Personality, 71(4), 495 - 513.

Castillo, C. T. (2001). The effects of a dual-language education program on student achievement and development of leadership abilities. (Order No. 3022340, ProQuest Dissertations and Theses, , 77-77 p. Retrieved from http://search.proquest.com/docview/251479399?accountid=7058. (251479399).

Centers for Disease Control and Prevention. (2012, June 08). Retrieved from http://www.cdc.gov/mmwr/preview/mmwrhtml/ss6104a1.htm

Charlesworth, R. (1987). Understanding child development. (2nd ed.). Albany, New York: Delmar Publishers Inc.

Chetty, R., Friedman, J. N., Hilger, N., Saenz, E., Schanzenbach, D. W., & Yagan, D. (2010, November 1). $320,000 Kindergarten Teachers. Kappan, 22-25.

Chickering, A. & Gamson Z. 1987, "Seven principles for good practice in undergraduate education", Reprinted by Honolulu Community College, National Learning Infrastructure Initiative, 2003, Mapping the Learning Space: Design Implications, Educause, viewed 23 March 2004

Clotfelter, Charles T. & Ladd, Helen F. & Vigdor, Jacob L., 2007. "Teacher credentials and student achievement: Longitudinal analysis with student fixed effects," Economics of Education Review, Elsevier, vol. 26(6), pages 673-682, December

Colker, L. J. Twelve Characteristics of Early Childhood Teachers. Beyond the Journal: Young Children on the Web, 1-6.

Cummins, J. (2000). Language, power, and pedagogy bilingual children in the crossfire. Clevedon, England: Multilingual Matters

Denning, S. (2007). The secret language of leadership. (1 ed.). San Francisco, CA: Jossey-Bass. DOI: josseybass.com

Dhuey, E., & Lipscomb, S. (2006). What Makes a Leader? Relative Age and High School Leadership. Economics of Education Review, 27(2), 173-183.

Do Kindergarten Teachers Make a Difference?. (2010, August 2). Retrieved February 21, 2014, from http://blog.columbiasocialenterprise.org/?p=1113

Eagly Johannesen-Schmidh and van Engen (2003) Transformational, transactional, and laissez-faire leadership styles: A meta-analysis comparing women and men. Psychological Bulletin, 129(4), 569-591.

Educational Testing Service (2012). Relationships between Big Five and Academic and Workforce Outcomes. Retrieved February 17, 2016, from https://www.ets.org/s/workforce_readiness/pdf/21334_big_5.pdf

Ehrler, D. J., Evans, J. G. and McGhee, R. L. (1999), Extending Big-Five theory into childhood: A preliminary investigation into the relationship between Big-Five personality traits and behavior problems in children. Psychol. Schs., 36: 451–458. doi: 10.1002/(SICI)1520-6807(199911)36:6<451::AID-PITS1>3.0.CO;2-E

Fox, Deborah Lee, "Teachers' Perceptions of Leadership in Young Children" (2012). University of New Orleans Theses and Dissertations. Paper 1546. http://scholarworks.uno.edu/td/1546

French, D. C., & Stright, A. L. (1991). Emergent leadership in children's small groups. Small Group Research, 22(2), 187-199.

French, D. C., Waas, G. A., Stright, A. L., & Baker, J. A. (1986). Leadership asymmetries in mixed-age children's groups. Child Development, 1277-1283.

Fu, V. R. (1979). Preschool leadership-followership behaviors. Child Study Journal, 9(2), 133-140.

Fu, V. R. (1970). The development of a nursery school leadership observation schedule and a nursery school leadership rating scale.

Fukada, H., Fukada, S., & Hicks, J. (1997). The relationship between leadership and sociometric status among preschool children. The Journal of Genetic Psychology, 158(4), 481-486.

Genesee, F., & Paradis, J. (2004). Dual language development and disorders: A handbook on bilingualism and second language learning. Baltimore, Maryland: Paul H. Brookes Publishing.

Goldberg, L. R. (1993). The structure of phenotypic personality traits. American psychologist, 48(1), 26.

Gravetter, F., & Wallnau, L. (2009). Statistics for the behavioral sciences (8th ed.). Belmont, CA: Wadsworth.

Gullo, D. F., Heroman, C., & Copple, C., (2002). Teaching and Learning in the Kindergarten Year. K Today.

Guthrie, K., Jones, T., Hu, S., & Osteen, L. (2013). Cultivating leader identity and capacity in students from diverse backgrounds. Hoboken, NJ: Wiley Periodicals.

Hahn, E., Gottschling, J., & Spinath, F. M. (June 01, 2012). Short measurements of personality - Validity and reliability of the GSOEP Big Five Inventory (BFI-S). Journal of Research in Personality, 46, 3, 355-359.

Hampson SE, Goldberg LR.; J Pers Soc Psychol. 2006 Oct;91(4):763-79.

Hampson SE, Goldberg LR, Vogt TM, Dubanoski JP., Health Psychol. 2006 Jan;25(1):57-64. PMID: 16448298

Henry, M. (1998). The Manager's Job: Folklore and Fact. In Harvard Business Review on Leadership. Boston, Mass.: Harvard Business School Publishing.

Hensel, N. H. (1991). Social leadership skills in young children. Roeper Review, 14(1), 4.

Hess, L. (2010). Student leadership education in elementary classroom. San Rafael, Calif: Dominican University of California.

Honigsfeld, A., & Cohan, A. (2012). Breaking the Mold of Education for Culturally and Linguistically Diverse Students. Lanham, ML: Roman & Littlefield Education.

Howard, P., & Howard, J. (2001). The owner's manual for personality at work: How the big five personality traits affect performance, communication, teamwork, leadership, and sales. Marietta, GA: Bard Press.

Irby, B. J., & Lara-Alecio, R. (1996). Attributes of Hispanic Gifted Bilingual Students as Perceived by Bilingual Educators in Texas. SABE Journal, 11, 120-143.

John H. Schiff, professor of edition at the Teachers College at Columbia University

John, O. P., Naumann, L. P., & Soto, C. J. (2008). Paradigm Shift to the Integrative Big-Five Trait Taxonomy: History, Measurement, and Conceptual Issues. In O. P. John, R. W. Robins, & L. A. Pervin (Eds.), Handbook of personality: Theory and research (pp. 114-158). New York, NY: Guilford Press.

Judge, Timothy A.; Bono, Joyce E.; Ilies, Remus; Gerhardt, Megan W. Journal of Applied Psychology, Vol 87(4), Aug 2002, 765-780. doi: 10.1037/0021-9010.87.4.765

Judkins Jr., P. A. (n.d.). Certain criteria lead toward leadership. Operations and Planning Rural Health Association, Farming, Maine.

Junn, E. N., & Boyztzis, C. J. (1996). Child growth and development 96/97. Guildford, CT: Dushkin Pub.

Karschney, K. J. (2003). Structured intergenerational dialogue: A multiple case study of eleven children in a leadership workshop. (Order No. 3106567, Gonzaga University). ProQuest Dissertations and Theses, , 261-261 p. Retrieved from http://search.proquest.com/docview/305278835?accountid=7058. (305278835).

Kirnon, S. N., & Pepperdine University. (2008). Inspiring citizenship and leadership: Youth citizenship seminar.

Lamon, C. C., & Valdosta State University. (2005). The impact of the Georgia Pre-K Program on the achievement gap between at-risk and not-at-risk students for kindergarten readiness as measured by teacher perception and student assessments.

Leadership giftedness in preschool children. Roeper Review, 4, 3, 26-28.

Lee, Y., & Recchia, S. L. (2008). "Who's the Boss?" Young Children's Power and Influence in an Early Childhood Classroom. Early Childhood Research & Practice, 10(1).

Lee, P., Lan, W., Wang, C., & Chiu, H. (2008). Helping Young Children to Delay Gratification. Early Childhood Education Journal, 35(6), 557-564.

Lester, J. E. (2002) Does Your Child Have Leadership Ability?. Ohio Leadership Institute.

Li, Y., Anderson, R. C., Nguyen-Jahiel, K., Dong, T., Archodidou, A., Kim, I. H., & Miller, B. (2007). Emergent leadership in children's discussion groups. Cognition and Instruction, 25(1), 1-2.

Lieberman, L. J., Arndt, K., & Daggett, S. (2007). Promoting leadership in physical education and recreation. Journal of Physical Education, Recreation & Dance, 78(3), 46-50.

Lord, Robert G.; de Vader, Christy L.; Alliger, George M. Journal of Applied Psychology, Vol 71(3), Aug 1986, 402-410. http://dx.doi.org/10.1037/0021-9010.71.3.402

MacLure, M., Jones, L., Holmes, R., & MacRae, C. (2012). Becoming a Problem: Behavior and Reputation in the Early Years Classroom. British Educational Research Journal, 38(3), 447-471.

Manley, M., & Northeastern University (Boston, Mass.). (2013). A mixed methods study on leadership, communication, cooperation, and collaboration in children enrolled in the learning leadership academy.

Markey, P. M., Markey, C. N., & Tinsley, B. J. (2004). Children's behavioral manifestations of the five-factor model of personality. Personality and Social Psychology Bulletin, 30(4), 423-432.

Mawson, B. (2011). Children's Leadership Strategies in Early Childhood. Journal of Research in Childhood Education, 25(4), 327-338.

Maynard, T., & Nigel, T. (2004). An introduction to early childhood studies. Thousand Oaks, California: Sage Publications Ltd.

Meriweather, S., & Karnes, F. A. (1989). Parents' Views on Leadership. Gifted Child Today (GCT), 12(1), 55-59.

Minnesota Early Childhood Teacher Educators. (1986). Kindergarten excellence: Knowledge and competencies of kindergarten teachers. St. Paul, MN: Minnesota Dept. of Education.

Murray, J., Theakston, A., & Wells, A. (2016). Can the attention training technique turn one marshmallow into two? Improving children's ability to delay gratification. Behavior Research and Therapy, 77, 34-39. doi:10.1016/j.brat.2015.11.009

National Society for the Gifted and Talented (2012). Giftedness defined - what is gifted & talented?. Retrieved from http://www.nsgt.org/articles/index.asp

Nelson, A. E. (January 01, 2010). In focus youth leadership—Stepping in early to grow great leaders. Leadership in Action, 29, 6, 20-24.

New Jersey Department of Education. (1999) Have Your Heard? The Truth About Kindergarten. A Guide to Understanding Kindergarten. url:http://www.nj.gov/education/ece/k/truth.pdf

Olivero, J. L. (n.d.). Leading leaders. Nueva Learning Center.

Piaget, J. (1952). The origins of intelligence in children (Vol. 8, No. 5, p. 18). New York: International Universities Press.

Pandya, A. A., & Jogsan, Y. A. (2013). Personality and Locus of Control among School Children. Educational Research and Reviews, 8(22), 2193-2196.

Parmer, L. (2012). The relationship between personality and leadership in adolescents. ProQuest Dissertations and Theses,, 201. Retrieved from http://search.proquest.com/docview/1283388608?accountid=7058. (1283388608).

Parten, M. B. (1933). Leadership among preschool children. The Journal of Abnormal and Social Psychology, 27(4), 430.

Prepared for Kindergarten: What Does "Readiness" Mean? Preschool Policy Brief for the National Institute for Early Education Research, 13-13.

Pramling Samuelsson, I., & Kaga, Y. (2008). The contribution of early childhood education to a sustainable society. Paris, UNESCO.

Rios, L. A. (2010). The relationship between emerging leadership behavior in children and their academic performance. Our Lady of the Lake University). ProQuest Dissertations and Theses, http://search.proquest.com/docview/866567855?accountid=7058

Rogelberg, S. G. (Ed.). (2006). Encyclopedia of industrial and organizational psychology. Sage Publications.

Rushton, J. (1966). The relationship between personality characteristics and scholastics success in eleven-year-old children. The British Journal of Educational Psychology, 36(The University of Manchester), 178-183.

Russell, B., Londhe, R., & Britner, P. (2013). Parental Contributions to the Delay of Gratification in Preschool-aged Children. Journal of Child & Family Studies, 22(4), 471-478. doi:10.1007/s10826-012-9599-8

Ryan, K., & Cooper, J. (2010). Kaleidoscope: Contemporary and classic readings in education (12th ed.). Belmont, Calif.: Wadsworth Cengage Learning.

Sacks, R. E. (2009). Natural born leaders: An exploration of leadership development in children and adolescents.

Scharf, M., & Mayseless, O. (2009). Socioemotional Characteristics of Elementary School Children Identified as Exhibiting Social Leadership Qualities. Journal of Genetic Psychology, 170(1), 73-94.

Schoenfeldt, K. R. (2012). Kindergarten program type as a predictor for reading achievement in third grade. (Doctoral dissertation), Available from ProQuest Dissertations & Theses.

Shaunessy, E., & Karnes, F. A. (2004). Instruments for Measuring Leadership in Children and Youth. Gifted Child Today, 27(1), 42-47.

Shipley, G. L. (1998). Early childhood educators' perceptions of kindergarten readiness in a southern Ohio school district: Implications for educational leadership.

Short, D., & Echevarria, J. (2005). Teacher Skill to Support English Language Learners. The Best of Educational Leadership 2004-2005, 62, 8-13.

Silverman, L. K. (2000). Counseling the gifted and talented. (1 ed.). Denver, CO: Love Publishing Company.

Soffler, A. A. (2011). What is the Nature of Children's Leadership in Early Childhood Educational Settings? A Grounded Theory. Fort Collins, Co.: Colorado State University.

Srivastava, S. (2015). Measuring the Big Five Personality Factors. Retrieved March 18, 2015 from http://psdlab.uoregon.edu/bigfive.html.

Stark, P. (Ed.). (2014, July 1). Glossary of Statistical Terms. Retrieved from http://www.stat.berkeley.edu/~stark/SticiGui/Text/gloss.htm#categorical

Texas English Language Learners Portal. (2012). Retrieved December 27, 2015.

The development of markers for the Big-Five factor structure. Goldberg, Lewis R. Psychological Assessment, Vol 4(1), Mar 1992, 26-42. doi: 10.1037/1040-3590.4.1.26

Trawick-Smith, J. (1988). "Let's say you're the baby, OK?" Play leadership and following behavior of young children. Young Children.

Villagomez, E. T. (2007). An inductive analysis of the self-perceptions of young children related to leadership as a construct. Our Lady of the Lake University). ProQuest Dissertations and Theses, http://search.proquest.com/docview/304717742?accountid=7058

Vygotsky, L. S. (1967). Play and its role in the mental development of the child. Journal of Russian and East European Psychology, 5(3), 6-18.

Wells, C. (1986). The meaning makers: Children learning language and using language to learn (1st ed.). Portsmouth, N.H.: Heinemann.

2013 Social Enterprise Conference, Columbia Business School. (2013, January 1). Do Kindergarten Teachers Make a Difference?. Retrieved, from http://blog.columbiasocialenterprise.org/

www.ingramcontent.com/pod-product-compliance
Lightning Source LLC
Chambersburg PA
CBHW060757050426
42449CB00008B/1438